# JUSTICE IN THE BALANCE

# JUSTICE IN THE BALANCE

## *Learning from the Prophets*

### JOHN L. MCLAUGHLIN

NOVALIS

© 2008 Novalis Publishing Inc.

Cover: Julie-Anne Lemire
Cover photo: iStockphoto
Layout: Audrey Wells, Christiane Lemire

Business Offices:

Novalis Publishing Inc.
10 Lower Spadina Avenue, Suite 400
Toronto, Ontario, Canada
M5V 2Z2

Novalis Publishing Inc.
4475 Frontenac Street
Montréal, Québec, Canada
H2H 2S2

Phone: 1-800-387-7164
Fax: 1-800-204-4140
E-mail: books@novalis.ca
www.novalis.ca

Library and Archives Canada Cataloguing in Publication

McLaughlin, John L. (John Leo)
    Justice in the balance : learning from the Prophets / John L.
McLaughlin.
Includes bibliographical references and index.

ISBN 978-2-89646-031-1

    1. Bible. O.T. Prophets–Criticism, interpretation, etc.  2. Justice–
Biblical teaching.  I. Title.

BS1286.M35 2008          230'.0411          C2008-906154-3

Printed in Canada.

We acknowledge the financial support of the Government of Canada
through the Book Publishing Industry Development Program (BPIDP)
for our publishing activities.

5  4  3  2  1     12  11  10  09  08

*In loving memory of Rita McLaughlin*

# Contents

# PREFACE

Many people think a prophet is someone who predicts the future, but that was a very minor part of the message proclaimed by Israel's prophets. The biblical prophets were called to bring God's word to the people of Israel. More often than not, this meant pointing out the Israelites' failure to live up to what the LORD required of them. The prophets' message was rooted in the Covenant that God had established with the people, which included laws about how they were to live in relationship to God and to one another. Those laws were given to establish a society characterized by justice, but far too often the Israelites fell short of that ideal. When that happened, the LORD would send a prophet to remind the people of their obligations under the Covenant.

Thus, the prophets were mostly concerned about their own time period. When they did speak of the future, it was usually to point out the consequences that would occur soon if the people did not abide by the Covenant. But the prophetic books are part of Scripture, and God's Word was addressed not only to those who first heard it, but also to us. This book seeks to understand the relevance of their message for believers today by first understanding it in the context in which it was delivered. Each chapter focuses on a single passage, considering what it would have meant for the people who first heard it, followed by reflections on how we can apply that meaning in today's world.

Some of the words and phrases used in this book may require an explanation. First, traditional terminology for the two main divisions of the Bible is problematic and has implications for how one interprets both of those sections. For some people, "Old Testament" connotes "antiquated," "outdated" and even "replaced."

"Hebrew Bible" is popular in many circles, but designating the material by its (primary) language of composition does not take into account the Aramaic portions of Daniel and Ezra or scholars' extensive use of ancient versions in other languages. "Hebrew Bible" also does not incorporate the deutero-canonical books, some written exclusively in Greek, which Roman Catholics and Eastern Orthodox Christians consider scriptural but Protestants and Jews do not. Similarly, "Jewish Bible/Scripture" is inadequate for Christians in general, for whom the first part is also part of their Scriptures. Finally, in any of these proposals, the second part of the Bible is still usually called the "New Testament," which implies that there is an "old" one as well. As an uneasy compromise, the terms First and Second Testament are used in this book for the two main divisions of the biblical literature.

Second, LORD is used in place of the name of the God of Israel. Even though the name is present in the ancient Hebrew manuscripts of the First Testament, a growing sense of the sacredness of both God and God's name, plus a concern that one might inadvertently take God's name in vain, eventually led to the practice of not pronouncing the name that was written. Instead, to this day observant Jews substitute the term *ădônây*, which means "my Lord," wherever the name itself appears. In keeping with this practice, "the LORD" is used in place of the divine name, but it is written in capital letters to signify that it is the divine name that is meant and not just the word "lord."

Finally, the abbreviations BCE and CE are used. These stand for "Before the Common Era" and "Common Era." They cover the same period as BC ("Before Christ") and AD (*"Anno Domini"* = "The Year of the Lord"), but the first set of abbreviations is commonly used by biblical scholars, especially in an interfaith context, as neutral designations that are not explictly linked to Jesus.

With the exception of Chapter 1, each of the following chapters begins with a reference indicating where the passage being discussed can be found in the First Testament. Reading *about* the Bible should not take the place of reading the Bible itself, so read each passage before reading the chapter. This book uses the New Revised Standard Version (NRSV) when quoting from the Bible, but any modern translation will do. Differences in wording among translations are usually the result of the various translators' choices as to how to render a word that has more than one nuance. Do not let that interfere with allowing the biblical texts to come alive for you today, which is the purpose of this book.

Kevin Burns, the Editorial Director for English Books at Novalis, encouraged me to think about writing this book and provided regular encouragement and guidance along the way. Anne Louise Mahoney edited my text with the superior level of sensitivity to language and attention to detail that I have come to expect from her through my two previous Novalis books. I thank them both sincerely for their roles in bringing this volume to fruition.

When I was in the early stages of writing this book, my mother passed away. She was a woman of deep faith who insisted that people be treated with respect and dignity. She had a special concern for the poor and the defenceless that would have pleased Israel's prophets. The contents of this book are influenced by her as well as by them, and I dedicate it to her memory with love.

*John L. McLaughlin*
*Faculty of Theology*
*University of St. Michael's College*
*September 2008*

# 1

## The Covenant:
## "Let my people go!"

The message of Israel's prophets is rooted in the Covenant. A covenant is any binding relationship between two parties, with mutual obligations. Modern examples include a loan or mortgage, a marriage, a political alliance, an international treaty, and so on. There are a number of "covenants" in the First Testament that spell out how the parties are to relate to one another. A covenant could be between two individuals, such as the one Abraham made with Abimelech confirming that Abraham owned the well at Beersheba (Genesis 21:25-32), or the covenant Jacob made with his uncle

Laban establishing the boundary between their respective territories (Genesis 31:43-54). A covenant could also exist between groups, such as the Israelites and the Gibeonites (Joshua 9). Similarly, God established covenants with a number of individuals, in which God made various promises. These include covenants with Noah (God would save Noah from the flood and afterwards promised never to flood the earth again: Genesis 6:18; 9:9-17), Abraham (Abraham would receive land, descendants and blessing: Genesis 15:18; 17:2-21) and David (David's children would rule in Jerusalem: 2 Samuel 7). But the most important covenant in the First Testament is the one God made with the nation of Israel as a whole. This is unique in the ancient Near East. Other nations often spoke of one or more of their gods entering into a special relationship with an individual, usually the king, but nowhere else do we find the belief that a god has done so with an entire people.

God's Covenant with Israel is rooted in the Exodus from Egypt. When the Israelites were slaves, the LORD intervened to set them free. This, too, was a radical departure from what most people in the ancient world believed about the gods. All ancient religions included a number of gods organized in a hierarchical structure, with a chief deity (who was always male), lesser gods under him, and servant gods below them. For example, in Greece, Zeus ruled over Apollo, Aphrodite, and so on, who in turned were served by individuals such as Hermes, the messenger god. Most societies were organized in a similar way, with a king at the head, a bureaucracy around him, the general population who did his bidding, and slaves at the bottom of the social ladder. People considered that particular social structure to be a reflection of the divine realm. As a result, any attempt to change the way society was organized amounted to challenging the gods themselves. This was even more the case in Egypt, where people thought that Pharaoh was the incarnation of Ra, the sun god.

But the LORD acted against such a hierar-chical model of society, intervening on behalf

of the lowest level of Egyptian society: the
slaves. This was a direct challenge to the belief
that enslavement was the will of the gods (or
God). Moreover, the LORD did not just reverse
the situation, putting the slaves in control, but
instead led them out of Egypt to Mount Sinai.
Once there, God gave them laws that established the Covenant between God and Israel,
specifying how they were to live in light of
their liberation from slavery. In turn, the Lord
promised to be their God, protecting and caring for them as "my people."

Contrary to popular perception, the laws
in the First Testament do not deal only with
ritual matters, such as how to offer a sacrifice
or what actions to perform when someone had
become impure. Such laws do exist in the First
Testament, but God also gave a large number
of social laws concerning how the Israelites
were to live in relationship to one another. We
can see this quite easily in the Ten Commandments. The first three commandments (Exodus
20:3-11; Deuteronomy 5:6-15) deal with one's
relationship with God, but the rest deal with

how people are to relate to one another (Exodus 20:12-17; Deuteronomy 5:16-21): they are not to steal, commit adultery, bear false witness, and so on. Thus, the Ten Commandments link our relationship with God to our relationship with others. The other laws elaborate on this basic insight. The "religious" laws indicate how to worship God in order to maintain a direct relationship with the LORD, while the "social" laws spell out how to act in relationship to one another as a further expression of the Covenant with God.

Underlying these social laws is the LORD's desire to establish a society that was very different from the usual state of affairs in the ancient world. God wanted the Israelites to live in harmony with one another, respecting each other as individuals made in "the image and likeness of God" (Genesis 1:27). To that end, many of the laws specify how the people are to relate to one another in their daily lives, always with a view to respecting the dignity of others. For instance, Deuteronomy 24:10-11 specifies that if someone borrows money from another, the lender may not enter the borrower's house to take anything as collateral, but must wait outside for the person to bring out the item, thus preserving the borrower's dignity. Moreover, verse 6 specifies that the borrower may not take a millstone as a pledge for a loan, since the person needs it to grind grain each day for bread. Verses 12-13 even mandate that if a poor person gives a cloak as collateral, it must be given back each night for use as a blanket (see also Exodus 22:26-27).

This concern for the poor runs throughout the First Testament. Three groups in particular are singled out for special attention: the orphan, the widow and the "alien" in the land. In a patriarchal society, it was important to have a male relative who could look after you, and especially to protect your legal rights. However, an orphan lacked a father to do this, and since a widow had left her father's house for that of her husband, who had then died, she also lacked a male relative to look after her interests. The third group, the foreigners, were not native Israelites and so did not have any

Israelite relatives, male or otherwise, to protect them. Therefore, to compensate for the fact that these three groups did not have a natural protector, the Israelite Covenant included frequent commands that they be protected (e.g., Exodus 22:21-24; 23:9; Deuteronomy 24:17-22). Those who had no specific person to look out for their safety and well-being were to be looked after by everyone.

At the same time, the biblical laws recognized that human beings are not always models of concern for others. Even the most compassionate individual can have periods of selfishness, or simply not be aware of the needs of others. To counter that possibility, the Covenant tradition included things that affected the very nature of Israelite society. For instance, interest on a loan was forbidden (e.g., Exodus 22:25; Leviticus 25:35-37). Interest can easily add up, making a debt grow bigger, often to the point that people can barely repay the interest, let alone the original loan. But because the Israelites were meant to live as a family, a community of brothers and sisters, they were ordered not to impose interest on their neighbours.

Nonetheless, drought, poor harvests and similar factors sometimes combined to make it impossible for an individual to repay even the original loan. In such circumstances, people were often reduced to what is called "debt slavery." In desperate situations, people would sell themselves to someone for a set period of time in order to get enough money to pay off their debts. The "buyer" would reap the benefits of the "slave's" labour, whether through working in the fields, at a craft or something else. But once again, the laws insured that this did not become a permanent situation. Every seventh year was a sabbath year, in which all "slaves" were to be set free and all debts forgiven (Deuteronomy 15:1-18). The text even encouraged the Israelites not to hesitate lending money if it was close to the sabbath year, and to give money and goods to those they released. The Jubilee Year took these principles even further. Every 50 years, not only were debts to be forgiven and debt slaves released, but any land that had been sold was to be returned to the original owner, or to her or his descendants (Leviticus 25:8-10). The goal was to ensure that land did not become concentrated in the hands of a few; instead, it was redistributed every 50 years.

All of this was a direct result of the Exodus and a reaction to the people's earlier state of slavery. God had set them free from that kind of life, and the laws God gave them were designed to make sure that they never had to live under oppression again. Thus, reminders that they were once slaves occur frequently throughout the First Testament. For instance, the first commandment says, "I am the LORD your God, who brought you out of the land of Egypt, out of the house of slavery" (Exodus 20:2; Deuteronomy 5:6). Similarly, the frequent admonitions to give special concern to the widow, the orphan and the stranger in the land are often followed by reminders that they had been slaves in Egypt (e.g., Exodus 22:21; Deuteronomy 24:18, 22). Exodus 22:9 even urges them to be kind to the stranger because they knew what it was like to be strangers in Egypt.

To summarize, biblical Israel was founded on the notion that God did not want people to oppress others, but rather to care for one another. The Covenant insisted that it was not possible to be in a right relationship with God *unless* they did look after those in need among them. Because God had set them free from slavery and oppression in Egypt, they were obligated not to enslave their fellow Israelites or those who lived among them. This meant lending money without interest, with no financial benefit to the lender. It meant forgiving debts at regular intervals and returning land that had been sold.

This says a lot about the biblical (and therefore God's) notion of justice. People often define justice as people getting what they earn or deserve, but in the First Testament, God commands the people to give others what they *need*, precisely because they need it. To make sure that happened, God gave them laws requiring them to do so, whether they wanted to or not. Of course, they often failed to live up to that ideal. That is where the prophets came into the picture. The prophets challenged the people to live up to the ideal society embodied in the Covenant laws that God had given them.

We live in a different world today, so if we want to take the Covenant seriously we need to make some adjustments. The ancient Israelites were primarily a rural people, living on small farms and growing their own food, while the majority of the world's population today lives in cities. The challenge for us is to translate ideas like the Sabbath Year into our modern situation. What would it mean to release people from their debts every seven years? What would be the equivalent of redistributing land in the Jubilee Year? Applying such concepts to our contemporary situation requires some creative thinking, but as we will see in the following chapters, the prophets insisted that those concepts remained valid for the Israelites throughout their history. If we take the Scriptures seriously as God's word to us as well as to them, then these commands remain valid for us today as well. After all, they are commands and not just suggestions!

# 2

## THE NATURE OF KINGSHIP:
## "YOU WILL CRY OUT
## BECAUSE OF YOUR KING"

### 1 Samuel 8

There are a few references to "prophets" in the early books of the Bible: Abraham is called a prophet in Genesis 20:7, Aaron is named Moses' prophet in Exodus 7:1, and Miriam is called a prophet in Exodus 15:20; there is even an unnamed prophet in Judges 6:8. But these are all isolated verses, and none of those people carry out an extended prophetic ministry. Moses is also called a prophet, but only three times, all of them in the book of Deuteronomy (Deuteronomy 34:10; cf. 18:15, 18).

Moreover, Moses does not function like the other prophets in the First Testament, but as a liberator and lawgiver.

The first long-term Israelite prophet was Samuel. Samuel anointed Saul as Israel's first king, and later anointed David as Saul's replacement when Saul disobeyed God. The emergence of prophets and kings at the same time in Israel is not a coincidence; it reflects the prophets' role as champions of Israel's Covenant with the LORD. A major aspect of their ministry was to remind people of the obligations that resulted from their Covenant with God, to challenge those who failed to obey, and to rebuke those who failed to repent. As we will see in the chapters that follow, since the kings often failed in this regard the prophets frequently spoke bluntly to the rulers. The episode we will examine in this chapter anticipates that fact by describing the nature of kingship itself rather than the actions of a specific king. In order to appreciate it fully, it is helpful to understand the reason why the Israelites asked to have a king in the first place.

Israel consisted of twelve tribes that traced their origins to twelve sons of Jacob. God changed Jacob's name to Israel, and "Israel" eventually became the name of the nation as well. They saw themselves as a large family descended from a common ancestor and united in their common devotion to the LORD as the God of Israel. Nevertheless, for their first two hundred years in the Promised Land, the twelve tribes were loosely connected and did not always act together as a single nation. For instance, the tribes did not always unite in battle against an enemy. Sometimes this was because they faced a relatively minor threat that affected only a few tribes, but there were times when Israel's very existence was threatened and some tribes still did not participate in battles (see Judges 5:16-17). The tribes even fought each other on occasion (e.g., Judges 8:1-17; 12:1-6) – once almost to the point of exterminating the tribe of Dan (Judges 20).

Still, despite such occasional lapses of national unity, for the most part the twelve tribes lived together as a loose confederation with no central authority other than that of their God. The book of Judges describes this period: whenever Israel was threatened the people would cry out to the LORD, who would inspire a "judge" (they were actually military leaders, not legal experts) to rally one or more of the tribes and overcome the enemy (e.g., Judges 3:9, 15; 4:4-6; 6:14; 10:6; 13:24-25). But each of these "judges" acted only in response to a specific threat. None ever tried to claim absolute authority or to pass on that role to their children. Abimelech, the son of the judge Gideon, did proclaim himself king after his father died, but he was mocked and compared to a thorn bush ruling over cedars. Ultimately, the people fought against Abimelech and deposed him from his self-appointed role as king (Judges 9).

This system of divinely inspired leaders in times of need worked relatively well for over two hundred years. But eventually, the tribes faced an enemy unlike any they had encountered before: the Philistines. Their pottery and language indicate that the Philistines migrated

from the Aegean Sea region of Greece. They
brought with them two inventions that posed a
great threat to Israelite independence. First, the
Philistines had weapons made of iron, against
which the Israelites' softer bronze weapons
were no match. Second, the Philistines had
chariots, which could easily overwhelm Israel's peasant army fighting on foot. In the face
of the well-organized and superior Philistine
army, the earlier practice of sending out a call
to the Israelite tribes and seeing who, if anyone,
showed up, would no longer work. The people
realized that they needed someone who could
unify them if they were to overcome this new
threat to their freedom, and perhaps their very
existence.

So they asked Samuel for a king who "may
govern us and go out before us and fight our
battles" (1 Samuel 8:20). But there were two
problems with their request. First, the LORD was
supposed to be their source of unity, the one to
whom they turned for support and protection,
so by asking for a king they were rejecting God
as their king (1 Samuel 8:7). If they wanted a

human leader to protect and deliver them, that meant they no longer trusted the LORD to do so. Second, a king would make them "like other nations" (1 Samuel 8:5, 20). But they were not supposed to be like other nations. They were supposed to be different! God had set them free from slavery to Pharaoh and gave them laws that established a different way of living together. They were meant to be equals, with no one dominating the others. Asking for a king meant returning to their earlier situation when they were subject to Pharaoh's rule.

Ultimately, God co-operated with their desire for a king. Later in the book of Samuel, the LORD guided Samuel in selecting Saul; Samuel anointed Saul, and later David, as king. Samuel even called Saul "the one whom the LORD has chosen" (1 Samuel 10:24). But before any of that happened, the LORD told Samuel to describe what life would be like under a king (1 Samuel 8:10-18). A king would take their children to serve in his army and in his palace. People would have to grow extra food to feed him and his officers, and would have to make weapons and clothes for them. A king would impose taxes of money, food and goods to pay for his wars and his building projects and to support his political ministers and military commanders. He would force the people to work without pay in order to build his palaces and fortresses throughout the land. They would, in effect, be his slaves (1 Samuel 8:17). Then they truly would be like the nations, but they would not like it. They would cry out to God, just as they had done in the past when they were oppressed.

It did not take long for Samuel's prediction to come true. Neither Saul nor David were as bad as Samuel said a king would be. But Solomon, David's son, was exactly the kind of king that Samuel described. Solomon established a large standing army, then demanded money and food to support it. He undertook great building projects throughout the land, and forced the people to do the work. Under Solomon, the tribes existed to serve him. They were no better than slaves under his rule – so much so that when he died, the ten northern tribes

rebelled against Solomon's son and established
their own nation. But they had not learned their
lesson, because once again they chose a king to
rule over them. And once again, this king was
not the LORD but a human being.

God did not resist giving the Israelites a
king simply because God opposed that particular form of political organization for a nation.
Rather, the problem was the social structure
kings created. As Samuel pointed out to the
people, kingship was very different from the
kind of society they had experienced for the
previous two hundred years. They had not had
a central government, and as a result they did
not have the things that tend to accompany
a central government, such as taxes, regular
army service, contributing their labour, and so
on. Moreover, in the case of kingship, power is
easily centralized in a single individual, which
can lead to arbitrary actions by a king who has
no superior to keep him in check.

That is why the prophets emerged along-
side the kings in Israel. The prophets were
God's messengers, sent by the LORD to proclaim

the Covenant, with its obligations to both God and others. A king could easily think that he answered to no one, so the prophets reminded the kings that they would have to answer to God. In fact, for the first few hundred years of prophecy in Israel, they usually addressed the rulers rather than the people as a whole. Only in the later years of prophecy did prophets speak to the general population; then, once the Israelite monarchy ceased to exist, the prophets slowly faded from the scene. According to Jewish tradition, prophecy ceased by about 400 BCE, although people continued to hope that prophets would reappear (see, e.g., Deuteronomy 18:15; Malachi 3:1, 23; 1 Maccabees 4:46; Matthew 11:10, 13-14; 16:14; 17:10-12).

Samuel's warning is still relevant today. Unfortunately, there are still dictators and absolute monarchs embodying the negative characteristics that Samuel described. But those living in democratic countries can also benefit from Samuel's words about the exercise of power. Sometimes democratically elected governments can think that their power is for their own benefit more than for the good of those they govern. This rarely takes the form of outright exploitation, but it can sometimes lead to laws that benefit those in power and their supporters more than the people as a whole. This would include taxation that puts an unfair burden on the poor in comparison to the rich, or labour laws that give an unfair advantage to employers while making the workers' conditions worse. Or it may simply be a matter of the party in power being more interested in staying in power than in doing what is best for the country as a whole. Whatever the case, just like the ancient Israelites, modern Christians are called to live as a model to the world of a different way of life. Whenever and wherever our leaders fail to act accordingly, we need to remind them, like the prophets of old, that we are not supposed to be "like the other nations," but rather an example of everyone working together for the benefit of all.

# 3

## David and Bathsheba: "You are the man!"

### 2 Samuel 11–12

In the popular understanding, David is often considered "a man after [the Lord's] own heart," even though that actual phrase only occurs at 1 Samuel 13:14. But the Bible does indicate a special relationship between David and God, such that the Lord promised him an unending dynasty (2 Samuel 7). This was not because David was perfect. In fact, David had many faults and failings: he could be proud, vengeful and manipulative. However, he was also able to accept his sins when they were pointed out to him, although most of the time he did need someone to point them out. More important, David not only acknowledged his sins, he would wholeheartedly repent of them. That is what made David special to the LORD: David's sincere acceptance of his sins and his willingness to turn to God for forgiveness, confident that God was merciful, but without taking the LORD's forgiveness for granted.

The most famous example of David's sin followed by repentance is his adultery with Bathsheba and the murder of her husband. As was often the case with David, he had to be confronted with his sin before he was able to acknowledge it and turn to God for forgiveness. The prophet Nathan challenged David about what he had done, but since David was the king and therefore a powerful man, Nathan raised the subject in a very subtle manner, leading David to condemn his own action without realizing that they were talking about him.

The narrator quickly sets the scene at the beginning of 2 Samuel 11. He says that in the spring kings went out to battle, and indeed David's officers had gone forth to defend against the Ammonites. But David stayed at home in Jerusalem. He was not fulfilling his obligation to lead the army in defence of the nation. This deviation from his normal duties foreshadows more wrongdoing.

Late one afternoon, David was strolling around the roof. This was not unusual, since a cool wind would normally blow in from the Mediterranean at that time of day, and many people would take advantage of their flat roof to enjoy the breeze. But since David was a king, he lived in a palace that was higher than all the other houses in the area. From that vantage point he could see onto the roofs of the other houses and even into their windows. While he was doing this, he noticed a beautiful woman bathing. He inquired about her and learned that it was Bathsheba, who was married to Uriah the Hittite, one of his own warriors who was away fighting on David's behalf. But even though David knew that she was married, he had her brought to his house and had sex with her, after which she went home. She later learned that she was pregnant, and since her husband was away fighting, she realized that David was the father.

When Bathsheba told David the news, he worried that his adultery would come to light, so he devised a plan to cover up his sin. He sent to the battlefield and summoned Uriah back to Jerusalem. After asking him about the war and the morale of the troops, he told him to go home to his wife. David hoped that Uriah would sleep with his wife Bathsheba, after which Uriah might think that David's child was his own. However, Uriah did not go home, but rather stayed with the king's servants at the palace. The next morning, when David asked why he had done this, Uriah answered that he could not enjoy the luxury of his own house and the comfort of his wife's embrace as long as his fellow soldiers were sleeping in tents.

Since David could not fool Uriah into thinking that David's child with Bathsheba was actually Uriah's, David came up with another plan. He sent Uriah back to the front with a message to Joab, the commander of the army. The message told Joab to put Uriah where the fighting was the fiercest and then have the others fall back so that Uriah would be killed. Joab followed his orders and Uriah died, just as David wanted. Then, after a suitable mourning period, David married Bathsheba, who eventually gave birth to a son. David had managed to avoid any negative consequences as a result of his adultery. People could think that the child was conceived legitimately, since David and Bathsheba were now married. The person most likely to complain, Uriah, could not, since he was dead.

That was not the end of the matter, however. The LORD sent the prophet Nathan to confront David about what he had done. Nathan knew that David had already killed one man to cover up his adultery. If challenged directly, there was a chance that David would kill again. So Nathan approached the matter indirectly. Instead of confronting David with his sin, Nathan told him a parable. Nathan described two men in a city: one who was very rich, and the other quite poor. The rich man owned many sheep and cattle, whereas the poor man could only afford one small lamb. But he cared for it deeply, raising it almost like a member of the family, such that "it was like a daughter to him" (2 Samuel 12:3). This is the first hint of what Nathan is getting at, because the name Bathsheba in Hebrew means "daughter of Sheba." But David did not pick up on that point, and Nathan continued with his story. He told how a visitor arrived at the rich man's home, but rather than provide a meal from among his vast herds and flocks, the rich man stole the poor man's only lamb and fed it to his guest.

Nathan's story worked. David was outraged at this tale of injustice, in which a powerful individual used his position to take advantage of a weaker person. David announced that the rich man deserved to die, and at the very least should repay fourfold what he had taken. But as soon as David rendered his verdict on the matter, Nathan turned the tables on him and proclaimed, "You are the man!" (1 Samuel 12:7). After acknowledging the injustice of the rich man in the story, David could not ignore the fact that he, too, had used his position of power to impregnate another man's wife and then killed the husband to cover up his sin. Just like the rich man, he had been without pity as he took a "daughter" from someone else in order to fulfill his own selfish desires.

Nathan drove the point home. God had made David the king of Israel in place of Saul, had blessed David with wealth and importance, and was prepared to give him even more. In response, David had broken two of the Ten Commandments by committing adultery and murder. Nathan announced that David would be publicly punished for his secret sin: his own wives would be taken from him by others and his household would be plagued by violence. David's only response was to admit that he had sinned. Because of this frank confession, David's own life was spared, but trouble did follow his family throughout his life and beyond. The immediate consequence was that the child born of adultery died (2 Samuel 12:15-18), and David's other children would prove to be a source of much grief to him later in life. His son Absalom killed his own half-brother, Amnon, who had raped Absalom's sister (2 Samuel 13). Later, Absalom led a rebellion against his father (2 Samuel 15–18). Absalom even made a public display of taking David's wives into his own bed in order to shame his father (2 Samuel 16:21-22).

The story of Nathan's parable illustrates the difficulty that prophets sometimes faced when called by God to confront powerful people with their sins. The king had the power to put a man to death if he did not like what the man had to say. Nathan responded to that dilemma by first disarming David with a story of injustice. Once David sided with the exploited man Nathan was able to challenge David to see that he had acted in the same manner. Today, too, people often use indirect means to confront those in power when they do not act as they should. An author might address a matter of social inequality through a play or a novel. Musicians write songs to protest against war or poverty. Comedians use humour, especially satire, to make people laugh while at the same time conveying what is often a serious message.

However it is done, abuses of power must not go unchallenged. Whether it is the rich exploiting the poor or the powerful taking advantage of the weak, if we wish to be part of the Covenant then we are called by God to speak out against these and other injustices we see. We might have to be creative about how we raise the issue, just as Nathan used a story to bring out David's sympathy for the poor man whose lamb had been stolen. But remember that Nathan did rebuke a very powerful person. The means of communicating is less important than the message itself, which is to point out when people's actions run counter to what God requires, in the hope that they will recognize that they have failed and then repent.

# 4

## NABOTH'S FIELD:
## "HAVE YOU KILLED,
## AND ALSO TAKEN POSSESSION?"

### 1 Kings 21

The Israelites often failed to meet the requirements of their Covenant with God. It is not easy to measure up to the ideal of a life lived in harmony with others. And if it was difficult for the Israelites, for whom this was their sacred tradition, handed down from God and their religion through the centuries, how much more so for those who were not raised in that tradition? Jezebel is a good example of what can happen in the case of a non-Israelite.

The woman's very name is used today as a
slur. To call someone a "Jezebel" is to charac-
terize her as a wicked woman, usually of loose
sexual morals. While there is no evidence that
the biblical Jezebel was promiscuous, she is
portrayed as evil, both for her general attitude
towards the worship of the LORD in Israel and
for specific acts of injustice in her life. The best
example of the latter is how she orchestrated
the theft of Naboth's vineyard.

Jezebel was the wife of King Ahab, who
ruled in northern Israel in the first half of the
ninth century BCE. She was a Phoenician
(modern Lebanon) princess, not a native Israelite. As such, she was not raised in the traditions
of Israelite religion, including the demands of
the Covenant and its requirement to act justly
in relationship to others. At the same time,
Ahab did not do much to teach her the religion
of her new home, but rather let her continue
to worship Baal, the god of her homeland. But
she did not just worship him in private. She
publicly promoted Baal worship on a large
scale, seeking to replace the LORD as the God

of Israel with Baal. To that end, she persecuted those who tried to remain faithful to the LORD and even put some prophets to death. Clearly, she had no interest in the God of Israel, and therefore no sympathy with the ideals that the LORD called for among the people. A God who had a special concern for the weak and poor in society, and called everyone else to share that concern, was foreign to her upbringing and stood in the way of how she wanted to live. She came from a society in which the rich and powerful held sway, and thought that their gods supported their actions.

Jezebel's attitude is reflected in the story of Naboth. Naboth had a vineyard in the Jezreel Valley, next to King Ahab's palace. Ahab wanted the land for a garden, so he offered to trade with Naboth for a better plot of land, or else to buy it outright. Naboth refused because it was his ancestral land. According to tradition, the land had been divided among the families of Israel, and this land was to be passed on from father to son. There were two reasons for this. The first was so that every family would continue to have a share in the land itself, reinforcing the connection with the others who also had a share in the land of Israel. The second reason was to ensure that everyone had a degree of independence. The ancestral plot of land ensured that every family had a place to live and to grow food. This principle was so important that people were forbidden to sell or give away their ancestral land, except in case of very great need. And in those cases, the Jubilee required that every 50 years all land was to be returned to the original owner if it had been sold (see Leviticus 25:8-17 and Chapter 1 above). At the same time, a vineyard was a common metaphor in the First Testament for the land of Israel itself, which belonged to the LORD (see Chapter 10 below). Thus, Naboth's vineyard had both personal and symbolic significance in this story.

So Naboth was following Israelite tradition when he refused to sell his vineyard to Ahab. Knowing this, Ahab did not force Naboth to sell or trade his ancestral homeland. But that does not mean Ahab was happy about the situation. Because he was the king, he was used to getting what he wanted. When he found himself in a situation where he could not have his own way, he did what most spoiled people do: he sulked. The mighty king Ahab went into his room, lay down on his bed, turned his face to the wall and refused to eat. When Jezebel found him like that, she asked why he was depressed. When she found out it was because Naboth would neither sell nor trade his vineyard, she was amazed! Her husband was the king of Israel, and where she came from, kings got what they wanted, even if they had to take it by force. So she decided to act in accordance with her own traditions and get Naboth's vineyard for her husband no matter what it took. She wrote to the elders and nobles of the area and told them to gather the local inhabitants for a fast. Once everyone was there, they were to have two "scoundrels" denounce Naboth publicly for cursing both God and the king. Although they should have protected someone in Naboth's position, the elders and nobles followed Jezebel's instructions to the

letter. The scoundrels also played their part
well, and Naboth was stoned to death for this
(false) crime.

Once Naboth was safely out of the way,
Jezebel told Ahab to go claim the land because
Naboth was dead and could no longer stand
in his way. Ahab was delighted with this turn
of events, so much so that he did not inquire
how or why Naboth had so conveniently been
taken out of the picture. He either did not
know or did not care whether Naboth had
suddenly fallen ill or been attacked by robbers.
His failure to ask about the nature of Naboth's
death suggests that even if he knew of his wife's
underhanded plot to have Naboth killed, he
would not have cared. All that mattered to him
was that he could now have the plot of land
that he wanted. So Ahab hurried off to claim
Naboth's land as his own.

But even though the elders and nobles had
not spoken up to defend Naboth, God did. The
Lord sent the prophet Elijah to condemn Ahab
in the very place that led to Naboth's death in
the first place: his vineyard. Just as Ahab was

inspecting his new piece of property, Elijah approached him. Every other time that Ahab had encountered Elijah, Elijah had criticized him for something or other, so when Ahab saw him this time he called him "my enemy" (1 Kings 21:20). Ahab knew what to expect from Elijah and he was not wrong. Elijah immediately condemned Ahab for what had happened, even if Ahab had not acted against Naboth directly and may not even have known what had happened to him. As far as Elijah was concerned, Ahab should have happily accepted the Israelite traditions that kept Naboth from selling him the vineyard in the first place. Jezebel acted as she did only because Ahab continued to covet the vineyard. If he had not, she would not have detected his bad mood and acted as she did. So Ahab was also responsible for what his wife did in order to get him what he wanted.

Elijah then announced a rather gruesome death for Ahab, Jezebel and their household. Elijah's justification for this rather harsh punishment is significant: it is because Ahab "caused Israel to sin" (1 Kings 21:22). On the surface, that does not seem to be true in this particular instance. He had certainly allowed, and to some extent even promoted, the worship of Baal in Israel, going so far as to build a temple to Baal in his capital of Samaria. But the murder of Naboth and theft of his vineyard did not involve the whole nation. True, the elders, the nobles and the two scoundrels did co-operate with Jezebel's plot, but that is not the same as causing Israel as a whole to sin in this particular case.

But on another level, that is exactly what he and his wife had done. They did not cause the nation to commit sinful acts, but they did open the door for the people to develop sinful attitudes. It was Ahab's attitude, his reaction when Naboth would not sell him his vineyard, that caused the problem in the first place. Jezebel noticed that Ahab was unhappy and so hatched her plot to have Naboth murdered. By refusing to accept the traditions of Israel that call for ancestral land to be kept within a family, Ahab indicated to the rest of Israel that it was all right to ignore those traditions and, by extension, other Israelite traditions. Similarly, when Jezebel arranged to have Naboth killed and Ahab did not investigate the cause of Naboth's sudden removal from the scene, he implicitly communicated that murder was permissible, and others could stand by and allow it to happen. By their attitudes, Ahab and Jezebel undercut the social laws of ancient Israel, the traditions that required everyone to look out for everyone else. The king and queen should have been models of how Israel's traditions could be lived out, but instead their attitudes and actions created the context that "caused Israel to sin."

There are a few lessons for us in this episode. We should certainly beware of leaders who might lead us away from the fundamental beliefs of our society and our religion. We must always be attentive to the actions of those who should be models for our behaviour. If they move in a direction that contradicts our community ideals, then we should be prepared to indicate our displeasure about the direction they are leading us.

At the same time, we must never lose sight of the need to speak up in defence of victims of injustice at the hands of the powerful. For instance, in ancient Israel the elders were responsible for ensuring that justice was done on the local level. But in the case of Naboth, they gave in to pressure from the queen, a more powerful individual. They should have refused to co-operate with her plan, warned Naboth of her plot and protected him from any further attempts to harm him. In fact, that was the responsibility of everyone in the community. It should not have been left to the prophet Elijah to denounce the king after the deed had been done.

So, too, we are called to be guardians of the weaker members of society. When the individuals and structures in society that should protect them do not, we must act ourselves. If the legislators, legal system, social workers, and others who should protect the poor and powerless fail to do so, then it is up to us to act on their behalf, both to meet their immediate needs and to challenge those others to live up to their own responsibility.

**5**

# Oracles Against the Nations: "For three transgressions ... and for four"

### Amos 1:3–2:3

Amos was the first Israelite prophet whose words were collected together into a book. Before him, people preserved stories about prophets such as Elijah and Samuel, which included at least some of what they said, but with Amos the emphasis shifted to his actual message. As the earliest of the prophetic books in the Bible, Amos set the stage for much of what follows in the later books of the prophets, both in terms of the message and how it is presented.

One example of how Amos's message was
formulated is found in Amos 1:3–2:3. Here we
find a series of sayings directed to foreign countries, which are known as the Oracles Against
the Nations. Oracles to and about other nations
are also found in Isaiah 13–23, Jeremiah 46–51,
and Ezekiel 25–32, but they are arranged differently in those books. In Isaiah and Ezekiel,
they appear between messages of doom to
Israel and messages of hope, while in Jeremiah
they appear after both types of oracles to Israel;
however, in the ancient Greek translation of
Jeremiah, they follow similar words in Jeremiah
25, reflecting the pattern in Isaiah and Ezekiel.
Thus, in those books the Oracles Against the
Nations are part of a pattern in which God announces judgment on Israel first, then the rest
of the world, and ends with messages of hope
and salvation. In Amos, however, the Oracles
Against the Nations come first. As we will see in
Chapter 6 below, they set the stage for Amos's
first Oracle Against Israel in Amos 2:6-16.

The Oracles Against the Nations in Amos
1:3–2:3 all follow the same pattern. Each be-

gins with the introductory formula "Thus says the Lord," followed by "For three transgressions of X and for four, I will not revoke the punishment." The reason for the punishment comes next, although only one transgression is mentioned, after which the punishment for this transgression is announced. In each case the LORD was going to send "fire" against the offending nation; in some cases this is followed by additional punishments. Most of the oracles end with the concluding phrase "says the LORD."

The six oracles are addressed to small nations that surrounded ancient Israel, with some identified by their capital city as representing the nation as a whole. For instance, Damascus (Amos 1:3) was the capital of Aram (v. 5), which is roughly identical to modern Syria. Gaza (v. 6) was one of the major cities of Philistia, the land of the Philistines, which lay along the Mediterranean coast but was not part of ancient Israel. Three other Philistine cities from this area are mentioned in verse 8: Ashdod, Ashkelon and Ekron. Tyre (v. 9) was in Phoenicia (modern

Lebanon); Edom (v. 11) occupied what is now southern Jordan; Ammon (v. 13) is now northern Jordan; and Moab (Amos 2:1) is central Jordan today.

As mentioned above, although in each oracle Amos repeats the phrase "For three transgressions of X and for four, I will not revoke the punishment," he actually mentions only one transgression. This numerical formula, known as the "x, x+1" pattern, was found throughout the ancient Near East and was a common feature of Israel's Wisdom literature. The numbers vary — they can be 2 then 3; 3 then 4; and so on; any combination of a number followed by one number higher is possible. There is a series of such numerical sayings at Proverbs 30:15-16, 18-19, 21-23, 24-28 and 29-31; other examples can be found in Job, Psalms and Sirach. Unlike in Amos, in the Wisdom literature such numerical sayings do list as many items as the second number named. For instance a "3, then 4" saying would contain four things. The final item in the list usually offered some kind of surprise or twist. For instance, Proverbs 30:18-

19 introduces "Three things … too wonderful for me; four I do not understand." The author then goes on to describe four "ways":

- the way of an eagle in the sky
- the way of a snake on a rock
- the way of a ship on the high seas
- the way of a man with a woman.

The point is to force the listener or reader to reflect on how the final element in the list relates to the other ones. Amos has adapted the formula to his purpose by mentioning only the final, climactic element, the major sin of each nation he addresses.

The transgressions of those six nations have something in common: each is related in some way to warfare. For instance, Damascus/Aram "threshed Gilead with threshing sledges of iron" (Amos 1:3). This alludes to excessive violence in battle: the soldiers of Aram went through a battlefield with their iron swords and cut down their opponents like a farmer mowing his crop. Gaza and Tyre are both accused of giving "entire communities" to Edom, a reference to selling prisoners of war into slavery. Edom itself is denounced, "because he pursued his brother with the sword and cast off all pity" (Amos 1:11). Edom was descended from Esau, the brother of Jacob (also known as Israel), so this indicates ongoing hostility between Israel and Edom, who were related by blood in the distant past. The Ammonites' transgression needs little explanation: cutting open pregnant women while seeking to expand their territory is yet another example of outrageous acts during war. Finally, Moab burned the bones of the king of Edom rather than allow for the proper burial of a defeated enemy, as called for by custom and decency. Amos's audience did not need any explanation to understand how offensive that was.

There is an additional point of contact between the third and fourth oracles. Amos complains that Tyre "did not remember the covenant of kinship" (Amos 1:9) and that Edom "pursued his brother" (Amos 1:11). The connection between the two is even stronger when we recognize that a literal translation of the Hebrew in verse 9 would be "covenant of brothers." In other words, at the heart of the Oracles Against the Nations is the concept of being a family. I noted just above that Israel and Edom were, in fact, related, being descended from two brothers. But there is no tradition of such a blood relationship between Phoenicia (Tyre) and its enemies. In fact, the oracle does not even specify which communities the Phoenicians handed over as slaves to Edom. Nonetheless, they have violated the "covenant of kinship." The prophet is not thinking of branches of a specific family tree, but rather the larger family that encompasses all of humanity.

This connects to another aspect of these Oracles Against the Nations. Although he speaks each time in the name of the LORD, the God of Israel, at no time does Amos ever refer to God's revelation to Israel. There is no mention of the Ten Commandments or any other part of the Law that God gave to Israel. Since the other nations did not receive that revelation, Amos could not have called them

to account for failing to live up to it. Nonetheless, he does call them to account. He clearly
feels that he has the right to condemn them
for their actions, and to do so in the name of
the God of Israel. That is because he bases his
accusations on "the covenant of kinship." He
assumes that all nations share a basic code of
conduct in relationship to one another, and that
they would recognize when one nation broke
that code, and even acknowledge that they
had done so themselves if it was pointed out to
them. That is why he thinks he can hold them
accountable, even though they had not entered
into an explicit Covenant with the LORD.

Philosophers and theologians refer to this
as "natural law." Natural law is the idea that
there is something inherent in human nature
that tells us some things are wrong. We do not
need to have God appear to us personally to
tell us that excessive violence is wrong. It is
taken for granted that killing civilians is wrong,
enslaving entire populations is wrong, attacking pregnant women is wrong, and abusing
the bodies of those slain in battle, even the

bodies of our enemies, is wrong. Today we call such things "war crimes" and "crimes against humanity."

Sadly, these acts continue to this day. The last century saw a series of wars that continued to raise the level of violence. In the First World War, people were shocked by the effects of new war machines such as machine guns and tanks. Unfortunately, the "war to end all wars" did not have that result, and the Second World War increased the level of violence. Not only did the means of killing improve, but it also targeted specific groups of people, leading to the extermination of six million Jews under the Nazis, as well as other groups such as gypsies, homosexuals, the mentally challenged, and so on. Soviet Russia committed similar atrocities, while more recently the world has witnessed "ethnic cleansing," children being forced to fight in rebel armies, and rape used as a tool to debase conquered women.

Faced with this litany of offences, it is tempting to conclude that we have learned nothing, and that humanity today deserves to be condemned just as much as the nations to which Amos spoke. We can take some small comfort in the fact that international bodies exist that do try to hold individuals responsible for their actions. There are at least some instances when people are tried for such "crimes against humanity."

Amos provides us with two reasons for hope in this regard. First, the Oracles Against the Nations provide a biblical basis for these efforts, reminding us that some aspects of international justice are fundamentally rooted in universal human experience, so that all can be held accountable. Second, Amos reminds us that even if we are not able to make such people answer for their transgressions, God can and eventually will.

# 6

## ISRAEL'S TRANSGRESSIONS: "THEY SELL THE NEEDY FOR A PAIR OF SANDALS"

### Amos 2:9-16

After six Oracles Against the (Foreign) Nations (Amos 1:3–2:3; see Chapter 5 above), and a seventh one directed to the southern kingdom of Judah (Amos 2:4-5), Amos turned to his main audience: the northern kingdom of Israel. Amos preached there around 750 BCE, during the reign of King Jeroboam II. Assyria (northern Iraq today) was experiencing a period of internal turmoil and was unable to continue expanding its empire for a time. As a result, smaller states did not have to focus as much on defending themselves and were able to use their resources for other purposes.

Thus, it was a period of peace and prosperity in Israel, at least for some. The upper class in Israel grew wealthier, but the majority of the people grew poorer. This fact is confirmed by archaeological excavations in Samaria, the capital of the northern kingdom. In the period immediately before Amos's ministry, Samaria consisted of houses that were roughly the same size as each other, but in the archaeological level from the time of Amos, one large house occupied the space where a number of houses had previously stood. Just like today, the previous inhabitants had almost certainly been forced out of their homes to make way for this "urban renewal." Moreover, the new, much larger houses contained signs of luxury and even opulence, such as ivory inlays and imported pottery, as well as other goods for export. But not everyone shared in this luxury, since smaller houses could still be found in other parts of the city.

The growing upper class that lived in these new houses depended on the lower class for its leisure and luxury. Initially, these were made possible by taxes that the king and his supporters imposed on the general population. Peasant farmers were required to pay these taxes even if there was a drought or the harvest was poor. In order to pay the taxes when they did not have many crops, the poorer farmers were forced to borrow money from the rich, who charged interest despite the biblical prohibition against this practice (Exodus 22:25; Leviticus 25:35-37). The rate of interest was high enough that the poor were usually unable to pay; lenders then foreclosed on the land, reducing the residents to the level of tenant farmers or day labourers. But they still had to pay their taxes. Some were forced to sell themselves or their families as "debt slaves" for a certain period. At the same time, there was a change in how the land was used. Rather than growing the food that a small owner needed to live, much of the farmland was converted to luxury items such as grapes for wine and olives for oil for the use of the rich, with the excess being exported in exchange for other luxury items for the rich. Meanwhile, the peasants were reduced to the bare minimum they needed to survive in order to work what had become the large estates of the upper class.

This was a far cry from the original ideal of equal members of clans and tribes, each owning a piece of land. In fact, it was a complete reversal of the liberation from Egypt discussed in Chapter 1 above. After the Exodus, the LORD had commanded the people not to charge interest. They were to forgive debts and release debt slaves every seven years. Each family was to keep its ancestral land, or, if forced to sell, was to have it returned to them every 50 years at the Jubilee. Instead, the rich had coveted the land of the poor, reduced them to slavery, and so had completely ignored the Covenant obligations that were supposed to be the basis for their lives. Amos was infuriated by this behaviour. He denounced the elite of northern Israel through a series of oracles directed against them.

The first one is found in Amos 2:6-16. It has the same structure and style as the Oracles Against the Nations in Amos 1:3–2:3 and the Oracle Against Judah in Amos 2:4-5. Like them, it begins with the opening formula "Thus says the LORD," followed by "For three transgressions of Israel and for four, I will not revoke the punishment." This was part of Amos's plan to lull his audience into complacency and get them to agree with him. The repetition of these phrases in each of the six Oracles Against the Nations and the Oracle Against Judah set up a pattern for his listeners. After the first few Oracles, they would expect to hear the same opening words. They may even have cheered Amos on each time he began the phrases again. After all, Amos was condemning foreigners, not Israelites. At various times in their history, those countries had been in conflict with Israel, so the people would have been glad to see Amos denounce them. Similarly, when he addressed Judah to the south, the northerners would have supported Amos. The two kingdoms had split almost two hundred years before, and the divisions remained.

But by agreeing with Amos when he condemned their neighbours, the people were setting themselves up for their own condemnation. As we saw in Chapter 5 above, the Oracles Against the Nations were not based on revelation. Those nations' transgressions were not sins against God's law but against natural law, and their actions would have been condemned by most civilized people as excessive and unacceptable. On the other hand, when Amos addressed Judah, he did invoke revelation. He condemned Judah precisely because "they have rejected the law of the LORD" (Amos 2:4). They had broken the Torah, the laws that God had given them at Sinai after freeing them from Egypt. But after agreeing with Amos that those who sinned against either natural law (the foreign nations) or God's law (Judah) should be held accountable for their actions, the Israelites could not then claim that they should not be held equally responsible when they violated both types of law. Nonetheless, they would have been surprised when Amos began the formula once again only to name them as the ones to be punished.

At that point Amos broke the pattern that he had used in the previous oracles. Instead of naming just one transgression, as he had done every time before, when he came to Israel he listed a number of offences. Some would fall under the heading of natural law while others were violations of the commandments in the Torah. For instance, the oppression of the poor and afflicted in the first half of verse 7 would have been opposed by most people in the ancient Near East. Similarly, although selling people (v. 6) goes against the commandment not to have slaves, there is something extra here that would also have offended many foreigners who otherwise accepted slavery. The verse says that "they sell the needy for a pair of sandals," which contains a double meaning. The Hebrew word translated as "for" can mean both the selling price or the reason; in other words, the text can mean both that they sold a person in return for a pair of sandals and that they sold

him because he owed a pair of sandals. Either
way, the sellers did not place a very high value
on their fellow Israelites.

On the other hand, some of their offences
were direct violations of a commandment. For
instance, verse 7 says that a father and son "go
in" to the same girl. In the Bible, when someone
"goes in" to someone of the opposite gender,
this is often a euphemism for sexual activity. In
addition, the phrase "so that my holy name is
profaned" indicates that a divine command is
being violated. Many scholars link the father
and son having sex with the same woman in
Amos 2:7 with Leviticus 18:15 and 20:12, which
prohibit a father and son from having sex with
the other's wife. But there is something more
involved here. In Jeremiah 34:16, the phrase
"my name is profaned" occurs in connection
with an act of injustice. A similar nuance can be
found in Amos 2:7 as well. The girl is probably
a servant who is forced to have sex in addition
to her designated household duties. The fact
that both the father and son force themselves

on her makes the exploitation of the poor all the more offensive in this case.

Another commandment is broken when "they lay themselves down ... on garments taken in pledge" (Amos 2:8). The final word ("pledge") is significant. Exodus 22:26-27 and Deuteronomy 24:12-13 state that if a poor person gives her or his cloak as a "pledge" for a loan, the person receiving it must not sleep in it, but rather return it by sunset, because a poor person would use a cloak as a blanket at night to keep warm. Amos condemned the rich for directly violating this commandment. The fact that they did so "beside every altar" (v. 8) heightens the offence, since it suggests that they were keeping a night vigil in a sanctuary while breaking the Law. Similarly, they drank wine in the temple ("the house of their God"). This probably refers to a religious meal eaten in the sacred precincts, which was a common event and not offensive by itself. But the fact that the wine was "bought with fines they im-posed" (v. 8) means that it too was obtained through the exploitation of the poor, rendering their ritual unacceptable to God.

Just in case his listeners missed the point, Amos reminded them of what the LORD had done for them in the past: the Exodus from Egypt, caring for them for 40 years in the desert, and destroying their enemies along the way. God had even given them prophets and nazirites, but they had forbidden the prophets to speak and forced the nazirites to drink wine, in violation of their vow to God not to drink alcohol (see Numbers 6:2-4). The LORD's past actions were the basis for God's Covenant with Israel, which included obligations for the Israelites as well as punishment when they did not live up to them (compare Amos 3:2). Therefore, because of their violations of both natural and divine law, God will punish them.

The gap between the rich and the poor has never gone away. Throughout history there have always been those who are better off than others. This is not wrong in and of itself. As long as everyone is able to live a comfortable life, most of us can accept that different people will have different amounts of things. But the reality is that there always seems to be some degree of inequity. In modern society, a small number of people own and control the majority of wealth and resources, while the majority of the population sees minimal benefit. In some places this even becomes a matter of built-in injustice, with the powerful able to ensure that society works primarily for their own benefit precisely because they are powerful.

This happens both within nations and internationally. For instance, Western and Northern societies consume a far greater share of the world's resources than do the other two-thirds of the planet. Moreover, these Western and Northern societies are able to structure the global economy in such a way that they increasingly benefit from the cheap labour and goods of poorer countries. People, including children, work for as little as a dollar a day to make goods that are sold elsewhere for hundreds of dollars, with the profits going to others. These people often work in conditions close to slavery, and are forced to continue to do so because of their poverty.

Amos would certainly have a lot to say if he were around today!

# 7

## THERE IS NO JUSTICE:
## "THEY HATE THE ONE WHO REPROVES IN THE GATE"

### Amos 5:7-15

After condemning northern Israel in Amos 2:6-16 for the oppressive society they had created, the rest of the book develops that message in greater detail by addressing different groups that contributed to the situation. In Amos 5:7-15, the prophet deals with ancient Israel's legal system, highlighting the way it co-operated with the injustice being done by the elite.

Amos called those who had corrupted the legal system "you that turn justice to wormwood" and "bring righteousness to the ground" (Amos 5:7). The wormwood plant was a shrub that was extremely bitter to the taste, and so was a common image for distasteful results (see Deuteronomy 29:18; Amos 6:12; Jeremiah 9:15; 23:15; Lamentations 3:15, 19; Proverbs 5:3-4). Justice should have been a positive thing for the weak, but it had become bitter to them. The law should have protected the weak members of the society, but in the hands of some manipulative individuals it had become a means of oppression.

Before spelling out how they did this, Amos reminded them that he was speaking in the name of the LORD. The God of Israel was not just their national deity, but controlled the entire universe. This is the one who made the constellations in the night sky, who controls the sun in order to produce day and night, and commands the great oceans of the world. Since the LORD is powerful enough to do all this, he can also punish those who deserve it, no matter how powerful they may think they are. The God who can destroy the strongest fortress can surely punish human beings.

Amos then turned again to those who perverted justice. They hated those who displayed the opposite traits, namely speaking the truth and correcting wrong "in the gates." The gate was the site where an individual would go to seek justice in ancient Israel. Entrances to ancient cities consisted of three or four gateways that could be blocked off in case of attack. Between each gateway, on either side of the passageway, were open areas, usually with benches around the walls. This was often the only large space in a village where people could assemble, and the elders would gather there to discuss the affairs of the town. If anyone had a legal complaint against another person, both would go to the gate and ask that their case be heard. There were no formal law courts with professional lawyers and judges, so the elders, by virtue of their age, were thought to have sufficient wisdom to decide all but the most serious cases, which would be taken to the king.

They were also expected to be impartial, but that was not always the case in Amos's day. The elders who sat in the gate were from the leading families in each town. However, the leading families were not determined by their piety but by their wealth. They were able to spend the day sitting at the gate discussing things precisely because they were wealthy, and did not have to work the fields or toil at some other occupation. But as we saw in Chapter 6, under Jeroboam II the rich became rich at the expense of the poor, through taxation, heavy interest on loans and outright exploitation. So the elders were in a conflict of interest; they were called upon to decide legal cases that benefited them. If they judged the harsh taxes and large interest rates to be unjust, they would be ruling against the very practices that had allowed them to rise to the position they currently enjoyed. Judges in Israel were supposed to look out for the rights of the weaker members of the society, but if they did so they would undercut their own position of privilege and power.

Instead, the judges themselves were unjust. Amos described their actions using language that echoes his first oracle against Israel in Amos 2:6-16. In Amos 5:11 they "trample the poor," just as in Amos 2:7, and impose levies or fines, as in Amos 2:8. They act against the righteous (compare 5:12 and 2:6) and push aside those who need their intervention (5:12 and 2:7). And lest anyone mistakenly think that they actually decided each case on its merits, Amos announced that they took bribes (Amos 5:12) in order to rule against the poor, who could not afford bribes.

These corrupt judges expected to share in the benefits that the winners in the lawsuits received, but Amos assured them that any pleasure would be short lived. For instance, they built houses of hewn stone as an example of their luxury. While stone was a common building material in ancient Israel, most people simply piled rocks upon one another to create walls and stuffed the cracks with mud and sand to keep out the wind. Only the rich could afford the luxury of hewn or "dressed" stones, which required stone masons who trimmed the stones to produce flat edges that could be neatly laid upon each other. As a result, there were few, if any, holes, and thus little need for filling. These were the kinds of homes that had replaced multiple family dwellings in Samaria (see Chapter 6 above).

At the same time, the rich converted the small parcels of land they had obtained by foreclosing on mortgages, and turned them into vineyards or olive groves. They had their own family land to grow food for themselves, so once they began to amass other property, they turned it towards the growth of luxury items such as grapes and olives. The produce could be used to make wine for their feasts and oil for cosmetic use. Any excess could be traded for other items, such as the ivory and pottery found at Samaria. However, Amos told them that they would not get to enjoy these things either. Even though they built luxurious homes, they would not live in them, nor would they get to drink the wine from their vineyards. Instead, the LORD of Hosts, the one

who controls all of creation, would hold them
accountable for their participation in such a
corrupt legal system.

But there was still some hope. If they turned
from their injustice and began to "seek good
and not evil," then they would live (Amos 5:14).
The LORD desires justice more than punishment,
so if they changed their ways and "establish[ed]
justice in the gate," then the LORD would not
destroy the entire nation, but would "be gra-
cious to the remnant of Joseph" (Amos 5:15).
Joseph, one of the twelve sons of Jacob/Israel,
was sold by his brothers into slavery in Egypt.
But Joseph rose to a position of power in Egypt
and so was able to save his family when a famine
occurred. Due to his prestige, the descendants
of his sons Ephraim and Manasseh became two
of the most important tribes in northern Israel.
As a result, Joseph himself often was invoked
as representing the entire northern kingdom
(e.g., Amos 5:5; 6:6).

We expect our justice system today to be a
true place of justice, and often it is. The courts
provide an opportunity to seek redress for those

who think they have been wronged. In theory, at least, it is possible for anyone to bring a case for adjudication and receive a fair hearing. Bribery and outright bias on the part of those hearing legal cases is not as big a problem as it was for Amos, although it does happen on occasion. The vast majority of judges and lawyers are honest individuals who apply the laws fairly. Nonetheless, it is still possible for inequities to occur. For instance, a single individual of modest means is at a disadvantage when suing a big company. Most individuals can afford only a single lawyer, whereas major corporations can hire legal teams to defend their interests. And while judges and lawyers do follow the letter of the law in such cases, sometimes the spirit of the law gets sacrificed. It is not unusual for big companies to bring multiple motions forward that draw out the proceedings. Sometimes it is possible to wear down a single opponent in this manner, draining her or his resources until she or he simply cannot afford to pursue the matter any longer.

Even worse, the rich and powerful sometimes influence the legislative system itself,
prompting lawmakers to enact laws that favour them over against the poor and weak.
For instance, in some countries the ability of
individuals to sue large companies has been affected, either by limiting the time during which
a suit must be brought forward or by granting
immunity concerning some aspects of a company's business. When this happens, justice
truly does become wormwood, and prophetic
voices need to be raised against such practices.
Perhaps we are called to be those prophets.

# 8

## Luxurious Feasts:
## "They are not grieved over the ruin of Joseph"

### Amos 6:1-7

In this passage, Amos addresses Israel's upper class concerning their complacent attitude towards the situation of their poor sisters and brothers. Amos begins by noting their sense of "ease" and "security" in Zion (Jerusalem, the capital of Judah in the south) and Samaria (the capital of northern Israel). They are the "notables" in the nation, to whom their fellow Israelites came expecting justice, but as we have seen, that justice has been denied. As a result,

God will punish the upper class for their lack
of concern.

Amos challenged their complacency in
two ways. The first is by the very nature of the
passage, which begins with the Hebrew word
*hôy* and consists mostly of a description of their
actions (vv. 1 and 3-6). While some English
versions translate *hôy* as "woe," it really has the
sense of "alas," as in the NRSV. The word comes
from ancient funeral liturgies in which someone
would lament the deceased by recalling that
individual's actions. Amos's use of the term
*hôy* has two implications. First, the actions he
describes will eventually result in the death of
those who do them. Second, by using the term
he acts as if he was preaching at their funeral.
Amos uses the funeral liturgy to convey that
they are already spiritually dead and that their
physical end is also certain, so much so that he
treats them as if they have already died.

After setting the tone of his message
through the word *hôy*, Amos also challenged
their complacency through a reference to
international events in verse 2. He mentions

three cities: Calneh and Hamath in what is Syria today, and Gath, one of the major cities of the Philistines. All three were significant cities, with Hamath even being called "the great," and yet all had been conquered: the first two by the Assyrians (from northern Iraq today) about 100 years earlier, and Gath, which had recently been destroyed by King Uzziah of Judah (2 Chronicles 26:6). If those cities could be overcome by enemies, Amos suggests, then so too can the capital cities of Israel and Judah.

Despite this warning, the Israelite elite had concluded that such an "evil day" could not affect them. At the same time, they brought near "a reign of violence" (Amos 6:3). Once again there is a double meaning in Amos's words. The Hebrew word translated here as "violence" almost always indicates oppression of the poor and weak by the strong, and so is an appropriate term to describe the effects of the elite's rule. But it could also apply to the actions of a stronger military force: namely, a conquering army. As we will see in verse 7, that is exactly the fate that awaited them as punishment for their violence against the weak and poor of their own country. Their own "reign of violence" over their fellow Israelites will result in a "reign of violence" against themselves by invading armies. However, at this point in the passage, the prophet's meaning is ambiguous.

In verses 4 to 6, Amos resumes his lament over their actions, painting a picture of conspicuous consumption at their feasts. He first describes them lying on "beds of ivory" and "lounging" on couches. The first phrase does not mean that the entire bed was made from ivory, but that it had ivory inlays and decoration. Nonetheless, this was still a sign of wealth, since ivory was not native to Israel and could be obtained only by trading food or other goods in order to get it from elsewhere. And as we saw in Chapter 6 above, ivory was one of the items found in the large houses in Samaria that had been built over a number of smaller houses. A second thing to note is that this is the only place where the Hebrew word rendered as "lounge" in verse 4 is used of human beings. Every other time it is used of objects that can hang loose, such as vines, curtains or turbans; a better translation here would be "sprawl." But once again, in keeping with Amos's method of holding back information in this passage, we do not learn why until verse 6.

A significant feature of their feast is the presence of meat on the menu. Meat was not a regular part of the diet in the ancient world. If a family was lucky enough to own an animal or two, these were usually kept as a source of milk and other dairy products as well as fleece (in the case of sheep), or for use in the fields (in the case of cattle). If people ate such animals they would not derive any long-term benefit, and so most people's diet was vegetarian. Thus, the consumption of any type of meat at the feast is itself a sign of luxury, but in this case, they were eating special meat. These were "calves from the stall" – young cattle that had been penned up so they could not move, thus ensuring that the meat was especially tender and did not include much muscle, which would have been tougher to eat.

These were very festive banquets that included much singing and music (v. 5), as well as copious amounts of wine. The NRSV states that they drank from "bowls," but once again the original Hebrew term sheds further light on the matter. The Hebrew word refers to the vessels used to catch the blood of sacrificed animals, which may have been as much as 30 centimetres across. This explains why they are sprawling: they did not just sip wine from small glasses as a pleasant accompaniment to the meal, but rather gulped it by the bowlful and thus got drunk.

The final feature of their feast that Amos mentions is the use of oil. Oil was commonly used in the ancient Near East for grooming; it was used in hair much like gels today and was also used to cleanse the body and help keep one cool. Amos specifies that they used nothing but "the finest oils," in keeping with their status. But as with all other aspects of their banquet, they use it without being "grieved over the ruin of Joseph." The tribe of Joseph was one of the most important northern tribes – so important that its name was often used to represent the nation as a whole. Once again, we have a dual meaning. In the first instance, Amos is referring to the negative effects of the elite's leadership on the people, especially on the poor, who are not receiving the treatment they deserve. But at the same time he alludes to the future fate of the nation itself, when the leaders are punished for their lack of concern.

That punishment is finally clarified in verse 7. They will go into exile, which of course requires that they will first be conquered. What Amos had been hinting at throughout the passage is made clear: "the reign of violence" (v. 3) that they were bringing near, "the ruin of Joseph" (v. 6) that they did not care about, is ultimately their own defeat by an army that will lead them away to a foreign land. Just as Calneh, Hamath and Gath had been conquered, so too would they. Moreover, there is a play on words where Amos describes the Israelite leaders as "the first of the nations" in verse 1, which in Hebrew is $r\bar{e}\,\dot{}sh\hat{\imath}th$ $bagg\hat{o}yim$. But now, the notable elite would be the first of the exiles, which is *rôʾsh gôlîm*. This difference of just a few consonants is even more striking when we note that ancient Hebrew did not write the vowels, just the consonants. And Amos was right: within 40 years, the Assyrians had solved their internal conflicts and resumed their military expansion, conquering northern Israel in 722 BCE and making it a province of their empire. Amos's use of the word *hôy* at the beginning of the passage was truly prophetic, because the elite's actions would ultimately lead to their death in exile.

It should be noted that although Amos clearly and decisively denounced the rich in this passage, he did not do so just because they were rich. Rather, he condemned them because they had become rich at the expense of others, making them poor. As noted in Chapter 6, Amos lived in a time of prosperity for a few at the expense of the many. We cannot know for sure what he would have said if everyone had shared in the success equally, because that is not what happened, but we do have a clear, explicit pronouncement of what awaits those who do not share with their needy neighbours.

Unfortunately, the modern world is marked by just such inequality, on a number of levels. The disparity between nations is obvious to all except those who blind themselves to it. And just as in Amos's time, this inequality results from exploitation of the poor and weak by the rich and powerful. North American and European countries are generally more prosperous than those in South America and Africa because the former have benefited from the resources of the southern countries. Centuries ago, the dominant powers simply took the material goods they wanted from their colonies, often taking the people themselves as slaves. Today, we in the North and West consume a far greater percentage of the world's resources than those in the South, often at less than a fair price. And even when we pay a fair price for our goods, we still benefit from the cheap labour provided by those in poor countries who have little choice but to work for as little as a dollar a day.

Turning closer to home, the gap between the rich and the poor continues to widen within Canada and the United States. Some live in mansions while others live on the street. Some go hungry while others have lavish feasts like those Amos describes. Some can afford to pay hundreds of dollars for fancy meals in luxurious restaurants while others have to go to food banks to survive until their next paycheque. Some company executives make 400 times what their workers make (compared to 20 times a few decades ago). Businesses themselves are often run with only one concern: to make more money for shareholders, regardless of the effect on the workers or the consumers. In short, our society is not much different from what Amos found in northern Israel 2,750 years ago. A clear inequality exists between those who are in control and those who are not, often with little concern for the latter.

Wealth is not evil in and of itself. But the biblical witness is clear that wealth is meant to be shared by *all* members of society, not just those who happen to have it. Moreover, when that wealth is obtained though injustice, it is simply unacceptable. Some well-known philanthropists use their wealth for the common good, and undoubtedly many more do so privately. But just as with the elite of northern Israel, God calls everyone to do something. No single person can change everything, but all of us together can change everything. Let us not be so dead to others that we die within ourselves!

# 9

## INSINCERE REPENTANCE: "I DESIRE STEADFAST LOVE"

### Hosea 6:1-6

Hosea prophesied in the northern kingdom of Israel a few years after Amos. Hosea's main concern was the idolatry of the northerners, who attributed their success to Baal, the Canaanite storm god. Since rain in an arid land such as Israel produces a sudden burst of fertility, the people mistakenly thought that the crops were a sign of Baal's blessing rather than that of the LORD, who had led them in the desert. Hosea reacted to this error by describing the Covenant relationship between the LORD and Israel as a marriage between a man

and a woman. Seeking fertility from another
god was comparable to a married woman having sex with another man: the Israelites were
guilty of adultery. Hosea was the first person
to use this marriage imagery, but many others
did so after him, right down to the present day,
when Christians speak of the Church as the
Bride of Christ.

Even though Hosea spent much of his time
and energy addressing the Israelites' worship of
other gods, that does not mean that the injustice Amos denounced had ceased, or that Hosea did not care about such matters. In fact, the
first actual oracles in the book deal with with
the nation's breach of the Covenant between
Israel and the LORD, which saw their relationship with others as part of their relationship
with God. After using his own relationship
with his wife as a metaphor for the relationship between the LORD and Israel in Hosea
1–3, Hosea calls the people of Israel to hear
God's word (4:1). The prophet presents the
LORD's "indictment" against Israel: that there is

"no faithfulness or loyalty, and no knowledge of God in the land."

In Chapter 16 below I will discuss the relationship between "knowledge of God" and justice. For now I want to highlight the nuance of the Hebrew word translated as "loyalty." The Hebrew word, *chesed*, is a prime example of how an English translation may not convey all the nuances of a word from another language. In the book of Hosea alone, in addition to "loyalty" in 4:1, the NRSV also translates *chesed* as "steadfast love" (2:19; 6:6; 10:12) and "love" (6:4; 12:6). Even within the span of three verses, the NRSV translates it first as "love" (Hosea 6:4) and then "steadfast love" (Hosea 6:6). Elsewhere, the NRSV uses additional terms, such as "kindness," while other translations add words such as "mercy," "piety," "favour," "loving kindness," and so on. It is clear, therefore, that *chesed* is a complex concept that goes beyond what can be conveyed with one English word or phrase. Nonetheless, despite how it is translated, the term is most often linked to the Covenant with the LORD and with other Israelites. The greatest example of *chesed* was God's entering into the Covenant with Israel, which is why the term is sometimes translated as "covenant loyalty."

The connection between *chesed* and the Covenant can be seen in Hosea 4:2, where the prophet specifies what he means by the people's lack of faithfulness, *chesed* and knowledge of God. He lists five of the Ten Commandments: swearing, lying, murder, stealing and adultery, followed by the summarizing phrase "bloodshed follows bloodshed." Of course, the Ten Commandments are part of the Covenant that the LORD established with Israel at Mount Sinai, and we should not overlook the fact that the five commandments that he mentions all have to do with their interaction with others, not directly with God. Moreover, Hosea 4:3 highlights the negative effect of the people's actions on the natural world around them, including the land, animals, birds and fish.

The issue of justice arises in a number of other places in the book of Hosea. For instance, in 5:10 he says, "The princes of Judah have become like those who remove the landmark."

This alludes to the appropriation of someone's ancestral land by removing the marker that established the boundary between plots of land, a practice that is frequently condemned elsewhere (e.g., Deuteronomy 19:14; Proverbs 22:28). Similarly, because the priests co-operate with such injustice, Hosea 6:9 compares them to robbers who murder travellers. Hosea 7:1 proclaims that Ephraim (representing all of northern Israel) has gotten rich through "false dealings," namely theft, while 10:13 refers to their wickedness and injustice, brought about through their power, when they should have been practising righteousness in order to establish "steadfast love" (*chesed*) throughout the nation (10:12). Finally, in Hosea 12:8, Ephraim announces that he gathered riches for himself only, with no sense that there is anything wrong with such greed. Taken together, these verses suggest that the prophet has been consistently referring to the upper class, continuing the pronouncements found elsewhere in the book against their unwillingness to share.

This brings us to Hosea 6. At the end of Hosea 5, the LORD announced that he would withdraw from the Israelites until they realized the extent of their sins and repented. This prompted the people's response in Hosea 6:1-3. They urged one another to turn back to God; since God had broken off the relationship they must go to the LORD in order to restore it. Unfortunately, their attitude was not one of repentance but of presumption. This is hinted at in verses 1 and 2 and confirmed in verse 3. In Hosea 6:1-2, they repeatedly state that the LORD *will* do various things to restore them to their former state: "he will heal us," "he will bind us up," "he will revive us," and "he will raise us up." At first glance, these phrases might be considered statements of faith, affirming their trust that God will respond to the prayers. But in verse 3, we see that they expect God to act on their behalf, regardless of their actions. They claim that the LORD will come to them as surely as the sun rises each day or as regularly as the spring rain that provides most of the water for the year in Israel. They speak as if God's return will be automatic, just like those natural events. But at no point in Hosea 6:1-3 is there a single word of repentance or any request that God forgive them. They seem to think that all they have to do is turn to God and God will respond. But they have forgotten that the spring rains, at least, do not come automatically. Sometimes there is a drought.

Their lack of explicit repentance provokes God's response, starting in Hosea 6:4. The LORD uses the image of water from verse 3 to rebuke them, but in reverse. He compares their "love" to a morning cloud that holds out the promise of rain but fails to deliver, and to the dew that forms overnight but quickly evaporates once the sun appears. The Hebrew term translated here as "love" is not the word for regular love, but rather *chesed*, which as we saw above was linked to the Covenant. At the same time, the LORD also reverses their allusion to the dawn; they took it to be an image that God *must* return to them, but he states that the rising of the sun melts away the dew. Their observance lasts no

longer than the dew, and it is precisely God's
presence that shows this to be the case.

God's words reach a climax in Hosea 6:6,
one of the more famous passages from the First
Testament (quoted twice by Jesus, in Matthew
9:13 and 12:7): "I desire steadfast love and
not sacrifice / the knowledge of God rather
than burnt offerings." Once again we find the
Hebrew word *chesed*, this time translated as
"steadfast love," pointing us to the covenantal
obligation that the Israelites must always care
for one another, and most especially for the
weak and the poor, which is precisely what the
upper-class Israelites were not doing at this time
in their history. This time the word is paralleled
with "the knowledge of God," and the rules of
Hebrew poetry mean that the two concepts are
directly related (again, see more on "knowledge
of God" in Chapter 16 below).

Hosea 6:6 indicates that in verses 1 to 3,
the people's words were accompanied by sacrifices as a means of restoring their relationship
with God. At first glance, Hosea 6:6 appears
to be very black and white: "steadfast love

and *not* sacrifice / the knowledge of God *rather than* burnt offerings." But this is one (of many) instances when we should not take the Bible literally. It was common in the ancient world to present a stark, absolute contrast in order to make a point. Thus, the proper sense of the verse would be to express it in relative terms, replacing "not" and "rather than" with "more than." The LORD is not calling for the abolition of sacrifice, but rather pointing out that it has less value than justice. It was certainly possible for prophets to reject sacrifice completely if it had lulled the people into thinking that God required only sacrifice. That point is made in much stronger language than here in Isaiah 1:10-17 and Amos 5:21-25 (compare also Jeremiah 7:21-24), where each prophet called for the abolition of sacrifice so that the people could realize that sacrifice cannot be a substitute for justice. But in Hosea 6:6, we do not have the same kind of extreme language, so it makes better sense to understand the verse as reinforcing the need for *chesed* ("steadfast love") as an expression of the Covenant, more than mere sacrifices in and of themselves.

The relevance of this passage for us should be obvious. If we have broken the Covenant with others, the way to correct that is not through acts of devotion or pious rituals, but by restoring the Covenant. Devotions and rituals are important, but they cannot and must not become a substitute for a proper relationship with others, as called for by God. If we turn away from those in need, then we also turn away from God, and we cannot repair our relationship with God without first repairing our relationship with others, since that is how we broke our connection with God in the first place. True reconciliation requires that we deal with those we have harmed in the first place, and when it comes to establishing a just society, that means those around us.

In Hosea 6, the LORD rejects the Israelites' attempts at reconciliation because their actions are not rooted in true *chesed*. In fact, reconciliation is necessary in the first place precisely because they have not lived up to the *chesed* called for by the Covenant. Worse, they tried to substitute acts of devotion instead of justice, when they really needed to make amends directly with those they had cheated and oppressed. That is why the LORD rejected them, pointing out that their *chesed* was transitory, and would not stand the test of time. God calls us to the same standards, requiring that our repentance be marked by an attitude of *chesed*, of care and concern for others. Better still, if we practised *chesed* all the time, there would not be any need for reconciliation.

# 10

# THE LORD'S VINEYARD: "IT YIELDED SOUR GRAPES"

### Isaiah 5

A vineyard was a common symbol for Israel in the First Testament. For instance, Isaiah 27:2-6 announces that God will always protect his "pleasant vineyard," which is explicitly identified as Israel. Similarly, Jeremiah 12:10 complains that the shepherds (i.e., the leaders) have destroyed God's vineyard, his "pleasant portion." But those other texts are probably based on Isaiah 5:1-7. Here, Isaiah sings a song about his beloved's vineyard. At first, the details make it sound as if he is talking about a real vineyard. When he identifies the vineyard as

Israel and Judah in verse 7, this is intended as a surprise to his audience. So it is likely that this parable is the basis for other vineyard texts in the First Testament, and by extension those in the Second Testament as well (e.g., Matthew 20:1-16; 21:28-32; Luke 13:6).

Isaiah introduces this passage as a "song." The passage is poetry. It is quite possible that the prophet actually sang these verses in order to get his listeners to focus on his message even more. A singer can reinforce the words by singing faster or slower, louder or softer, and so on. It is often easier to convey emotion through song than with spoken words only, and emotion is a key part of this passage. Isaiah says that he is singing on behalf of his "beloved" (v. 1). This indicates a close relationship between the prophet and this individual, but his audience would not necessarily know who the person was. As we will see, this deep connection between the beloved and Isaiah also extends to the beloved and the vineyard. It soon becomes obvious why Isaiah calls this a "love-song" in verse 1.

Isaiah tells us that his beloved had a vineyard. It was not just any piece of land, but was "on a very fertile hill" (v. 1). This raises expectations that it would produce a large crop of high quality, and the owner undertook a number of actions to guarantee that outcome. He tilled the ground and removed any stones that were in the field to ensure that his vines would be planted in the best possible soil, without rocks to interfere with the roots. Then he planted his vineyard with "choice vines"; Isaiah emphasizes the quality of the vines, once again conveying the care and concern that the vineyard owner had for the vineyard. The owner also built a wall around the vineyard (v. 5) to keep out those who might trample the vines or eat the produce before the harvest, and built a watchtower from which to watch for any intruders who made it past the wall. Finally, he prepared a wine press because he expected the vineyard to yield grapes that would be good enough to be made into wine. After all, he had gone to great effort to prepare the vineyard and protect it. Then he would have waited for several years, because it takes a few harvests before vines produce grapes of sufficient quality to make wine. But when it came time to harvest the grapes for wine, the vineyard failed to meet his expectation or repay his care and concern. All it produced was wild grapes, unsuitable for anything other than to be thrown away.

At this point the vineyard owner himself began to speak, addressing the people of Judah and Jerusalem and asking them to make a judgment on the situation. He wondered if there was anything else that he could possibly have done to ensure a harvest of quality grapes. The expected answer would be "no." So he described what he was going to do to this vineyard that had not repaid his careful tending. He would abandon it. He would tear down its hedge wall so that it would no longer be separated from the surrounding land. People would be able to walk across it without any obstacles, and so would trample any remnants of the vines. It would no longer be cultivated, but rather would become overgrown with briers and thorns. Finally, he would not let the clouds rain upon it.

At this point, Isaiah's audience would have realized that this was no ordinary landowner, because no human being can control the rain, never mind with such precision. Then in verse 7, Isaiah speaks in his own voice again, clarifying that the vineyard owner is the LORD and that the vineyard is a symbol of Israel and Judah. They were "his pleasant planting" (note this phrase at Isaiah 27:2-6 as well), and the wild grapes the vineyard produced stand for their evil deeds. Just as the vineyard owner expected the land to produce grapes but it brought forth wild grapes, so too the LORD expected his Covenant people to produce justice and righteousness but instead God found bloodshed and a cry of distress from the oppressed. The Lord's disappointment is effectively conveyed through similar sounding words. The LORD expected to find *mishpat* (justice) but instead saw *mispach* (bloodshed); he desired *tsedaqah* (righteousness) but instead heard *tse'aqah* (a cry). This play on words reinforces the contrast between what the LORD desired and what the people did.

Isaiah elaborated on this song with a series
of oracles beginning with the Hebrew word *hôy*
(Isaiah 5:8, 11, 18, 20, 21, 22) and followed
by a reference to individuals doing various
things that produce the bloodshed or outcry
that was denounced in the song. The NRSV
translates *hôy* here as "Ah." Other versions use
"woe," but it really has the sense of "alas," as we
saw at Amos 6:1 (see Chapter 8 above). Just
like Amos, Isaiah uses this word from ancient
funeral liturgies to emphasize that his audience
is spiritually dead, and that the punishment for
their actions will be physical death.

Each of the "Alas" sayings addresses individuals who do things that result in bloodshed
or produce a cry for help from those they
are harming. This is then followed by an announcement of their punishment, which fits
their offence by reversing their deeds. For
instance, verse 8 laments those who bought
land to create large estates while driving small,
poor farmers from their land, all in violation
of the traditions concerning the preservation
of ancestral land (see Chapter 4 above). In re-

sponse, Isaiah announced that their own houses would be deserted and their estates would not yield a normal harvest. Similarly, in verse 11, the prophet says "alas" concerning those who live a life of luxury, spending each day at great feasts marked by much drinking, eating and music, but not looking to see what God wanted them to do (v. 12). As a result, they will go into exile where they will experience great hunger and thirst.

Starting in verse 18, the "alas statements" are not immediately followed by an announcement of punishment. Instead, they come one after another in verses 18, 20, 21 and 22. Their punishment is then described at length in verses 24 to 30. This arrangement creates a sense of urgency as one offence after another is described in rapid succession. These offences are also the opposite of the justice and righteousness that the LORD desired, and include sinning while mocking God for failing to act, pretending that evil deeds are good and vice versa, acting out of self-importance rather than humility before God and perverting justice in the law courts. Isaiah assures them that God will punish them for all their sins.

God's basic expectations do not change. What the LORD expected from the ancient Israelites, the LORD also expects from us today: justice and righteousness. Unfortunately, all too often God finds bloodshed and an outcry in the modern world. This can range from the large-scale violence of warfare in a number of places around the world, to instances of oppressive regimes using force to prevent protests, to individual murders. Even when there is no outright violence, there are still many forms of oppression, such as discrimination based on how someone looks or acts, or manipulation of economic affairs by the rich to increase their wealth at the expense of the poor. Every kind of activity Isaiah mentions in his "alas" sayings can be found today: land-grabbing, lifestyles marked by conspicuous consumption, bribery in legal cases, and so on. And these do not just occur in far away places, but in our own country as well.

Since those offences still occur, Isaiah's warning about the consequences of such actions also applies today. God notices such things, and God will judge people accordingly. But we should not despair. Three different points from Isaiah 5 give us reason to hope. First, the passage is not concerned with minor transgressions, but serious offences against the Covenant with God and others. Second, God does not punish indiscriminately, but rather deals with those who sin, treating them accordingly. Third, the Love-song of the Vineyard stresses the LORD's devotion to the vineyard. Isaiah goes out of his way to emphasize the many things the LORD does for the vineyard in order to prepare it to produce good fruit. We can and should assume that God does the same with and for us. Moreover, we can expect to encounter that same attitude from God if and when we repent.

# 11

# Unjust Laws:
## "Alas, you who make iniquitous decrees"

### Isaiah 10:1-4

In Chapter 10, Isaiah resumes the "alas" form that he used in Isaiah 5. Once again he laments the actions of a group of people and warns them of the consequences if they do not repent. In Isaiah 5:22, he lamented judges who took bribes from the rich, thereby depriving the innocent of justice. Here, too, he is concerned with legal affairs, but this time his focus is on legislators. Specifically, his target is those who created unjust laws (Isaiah 10:1) despite the requirements of the Covenant embodied in the Law of Moses. Unjust lawmakers are different from people who manipulate and distort good laws. Laws should protect the weak and ensure that society as a whole is characterized by justice and right relations. It is always possible that someone could interpret a law that was formulated with the best of intentions in such a way as to provide an unfair advantage, but in most cases, that would be contrary to what the legislators intended. Judges and the legal system itself are supposed to ensure that such a thing does not happen and to provide relief when it does.

But what happens when people intentionally create bad laws, laws that favour one group over another? This is exactly the situation Isaiah faced. He does not specify exactly what the "iniquitous decrees" and "oppressive statutes" were, but we can get some idea from the people who were negatively affected by them: the needy, the poor, widows and orphans. It is safe to assume that laws that were bad for such people were good for their opposite: the rich and powerful. This stands to reason, since

those making the laws in Israel would themselves have been numbered among the rulers
and the upper class. At the same time, based
on the concerns raised in Isaiah 5 (see Chapter
10 above), it is likely that similar offences are
involved here. Therefore, Isaiah was probably
objecting to laws concerned with financial
matters, such as excessive interest on loans,
giving preferential treatment to lenders so that
they could easily foreclose on mortgages, and
limiting the right of those affected to appeal
to the courts for help.

At first, Isaiah uses two general terms for
the people being exploited by these unjust
laws, but then he identifies two specific groups
as well. Speaking in the LORD's name, he starts
with the "needy" and the "poor," adding in the
second case that they are "my people." This
should have reminded Isaiah's audience of the
Covenant that God made with the people of
Israel after the Exodus, in which they became
"his people." In turn, the Covenant should have
called to mind the fact that it required them to
care for everyone in the Covenant community,

but especially the weakest and most in need of help.

Isaiah then identifies widows and orphans as two groups affected by these evil laws. This, too, should have had special significance for Isaiah's audience. In Chapter 1 above we saw that widows and orphans were two of three groups who were singled out for special attention in the First Testament. (The third was foreigners.) It is significant that the frequent commands to care for these three groups of people who did not have anyone to protect them are usually followed by a reminder that the Israelites had once been strangers in Egypt, "that house of slavery" (see, for example, Deuteronomy 25:17-18). In Egypt, the Israelites did not enjoy the usual means of legal protection, and so were enslaved by Pharaoh. Therefore, they were told to remember their previous state, and make sure that they did not do the same to others, whether through physical force or legal corruption. Just as the LORD had entered into a Covenant with them after freeing them from Egypt, so too they were to enter into a Covenant with one another, and especially with the weakest among them, to ensure that others did not become enslaved.

The unjust legislators were not living up to this obligation, but were actually doing the opposite. They were intentionally creating laws that afflicted the poor and needy, and preyed on orphans and widows. Therefore, Isaiah singled out these nobles and the upper class for special condemnation. As he did many other times, he reminded them that their day of punishment would eventually come in the form of foreign conquerors, and that they would not be able to escape it. Moreover, since they had failed to live up to the Covenant ideals that God required of them, they could not expect God's protection, since the conquering army would be the agent of God's anger toward them.

Most modern countries are blessed with honest, just legislators who seek what is best for their country as a whole. Fortunately, there are few instances of lawmakers who are blatantly corrupt and consciously try to exploit the weak and the poor. And in a democracy, at least, we would hope such people would not get re-elected. But that does not mean that Isaiah's message is irrelevant today. Any observer of the political world knows that there are still exceptions who implement negative laws. There are occasions when legislators become greedy and accept bribes or other benefits in order to influence legislation on behalf of one group or another.

But even when a legislative body is totally free of such corruption, we still should not become complacent. For instance, the North American system includes lobbyists who seek to persuade lawmakers to enact laws favourable to the group the lobbyist represents. There is nothing illegal about that, in and of itself, but we must remember that lobbyists get paid, and the poor cannot afford to hire lobbyists to speak for them in the halls of power. Similarly, different political parties have different views about how the country should be run, and make laws in keeping with those views. While those views are honestly held, we must be attentive to what effect they may have when put into practice.

So how do we know whether modern laws are "iniquitous" or "oppressive"? The best approach is to consider their effect on those people Isaiah mentions: the needy, the poor, the orphans, the widows. Just as they were singled out for special attention in ancient Israel, we should also be concerned about them and look out for their well-being. If a law has a negative effect on the weaker members of society, those least able to defend themselves, then it is our responsibility to defend them ourselves. That may mean opposing a law that benefits us if at the same time it harms the vulnerable. Doing so may not be convenient for me, but that is what it means to have a Covenant with my brothers and sisters around me.

# 12

## An Ideal King:
## "He shall not judge
## by what his eyes see"
### Isaiah 11:1-9

In its present position in the book of Isaiah, this passage is probably meant to celebrate the coming rule of King Hezekiah, who reigned in Jerusalem from 715–687 BCE. It may have been composed at the time of his birth, but more likely it stems from when he actually took the throne at the age of 25. The book of Isaiah contrasts Hezekiah with his father, Ahaz, a rebellious king who would not follow Isaiah's advice from the LORD. For instance, when Judah was attacked by northern Israel and Syria in

734 BCE, Isaiah urged Ahaz to trust in God's holy presence in Jerusalem. Since the Temple was in Jerusalem, Isaiah promised Ahaz that the LORD was also present to protect the city and all those inside it. As a sign of God's presence, Isaiah gave Ahaz the famous prophecy of a child named Immanuel (Isaiah 7:14), a Hebrew word meaning "God is with us." Isaiah assured Ahaz that before that child was weaned, the kings attacking him would be gone. The immediate fulfillment of that prophecy was Ahaz's son Hezekiah. All Ahaz had to do was be humble and accept God's protection. But Ahaz rejected Isaiah's advice and instead asked the Assyrians (from what is northern Iraq today) for military assistance. The Assyrians did force the other kings to withdraw from Jerusalem, but at the same time Judah became subject to Assyrian oversight.

In contrast to his father, Hezekiah was a model of faithfulness. In fact, Hezekiah is one of only three kings from Israel's entire history who received a positive evaluation in the Bible (2 Kings 18:3-7; the other two were Asa

[1 Kings 15:11-14] and Josiah [2 Kings 22:2; 23:25]). The main reason for this is that Hezekiah reformed Israel's religion in order to do away with any objects or practices that might distract the people from their proper devotion to the LORD. But he also rejected Assyrian control, leading the Assyrians to attack Jerusalem. Thus, Hezekiah faced the same military situation as Ahaz had faced many years before. But unlike his father, Hezekiah did not appeal to a foreign power to protect him from these invaders. Instead, he followed Isaiah's advice to trust in the LORD's presence among the Israelites. As a result, God intervened against the Assyrians, who withdrew to their homeland. In contrast to his father's pride, which led to Israel's subordination to Assyria for decades, Hezekiah's humble trust in the LORD's ability to protect him and his people meant that the nation did not fall to the invading Assyrians, but rather regained a degree of independence.

This poem celebrates Hezekiah in glowing terms. Right at the beginning, he is associated with David, Israel's second king, who had followed after the LORD's heart (1 Samuel 13:14; see Chapter 2 above). Hezekiah is from "the stump of Jesse" and "out of his roots" (Isaiah 11:1). Since Jesse was David's father, this calls to mind both David and David's own religious roots in the Law of God and the land God gave to Israel. Similarly, Hezekiah is a "shoot" and a "branch" that emerges from these elements of Israel's traditions. Thus, this imagery of a tree reminds us that God's blessings on Israel were an ongoing, life-giving process, not just something that happened in the past. Hezekiah represented God's continued presence among the people through continuity with David as well as through Hezekiah's own experience of the LORD's presence in his life. The people can expect what happened with David to continue with Hezekiah.

That is because "the spirit of the LORD shall rest on him" (Isaiah 11:2). The choice of the verb "rest" is significant, because it conveys a sense of ongoing presence. The spirit does not just "come upon" Hezekiah or "anoint" him or "inspire" him; it *rests* upon him. Someone

could misinterpret any of the first set of verbs
as implying one phase in Hezekiah's life. By
saying that the spirit shall "rest" on Hezekiah,
the poet emphasizes that it will remain with
him as an ongoing sign of God's presence. The
qualities the spirit imparts are also important.
The Hebrew text lists six sets of pairs: "wisdom
and understanding," "counsel and might" and
"knowledge and the fear of the LORD." Each of
these characteristics is necessary if the king is
going to rule properly, making decisions for
the benefit of the whole people rather than just
himself and those close to him.

The ancient Greek translation of the First
Testament includes a seventh quality: piety.
When this is added, we get the traditional list
of the seven gifts of the Holy Spirit. This is not
just an accidental addition, however. The Hebrew lists ends with "fear of the LORD," which
is emphasized in the next verse: "his delight
shall be in the fear of the LORD" (Isaiah 11:3).
The fear of the LORD is an important concept
in the First Testament. For example, Proverbs
9:10 says, "the fear of the LORD is the beginning

of wisdom" (see also Proverbs 1:7; Job 28:28;
Sirach 1:14; Psalm 111:10). And as Solomon
demonstrated when he became king, a king
needs wisdom more than power or riches to
govern properly (1 Kings 3:5-14). But "fear of
the LORD" is often misunderstood to mean that
we should be afraid of God, which is contrary
to the repeated biblical affirmations that God
is loving and merciful. In this phrase, the Hebrew term rendered as "fear" has the sense of
"awe" – an attitude of respect in relationship to
a great and powerful God who has chosen the
Israelites to be his special people. Thus, the
phrase "the fear of the LORD" would be better
translated as "religion." And the practice of
good religion – namely, adopting a proper attitude towards God – is what we mean by the
word "piety."

Hezekiah's attitude is expressed in how
he judges (v. 3). He does not make decisions
on the basis of appearances ("by what his eyes
see") or what is reported to him ("by what his
ears hear"). Instead, his judgments will be based
on righteousness and equity, with a special

emphasis on the poor and the meek. In fact, righteousness and faithfulness will be like his belt: something that surrounds him every day as he goes about his royal duties.

The result sounds like a return to the Garden of Eden. Animals that hunt one another as prey will live together in peace, with a child to lead them. This is similar to Adam naming all the animals in the Garden, with no evidence of conflict among them, or between them and human beings. However, after the Flood, the LORD gave humans permission to eat animals, with the result that from that time forward, animals would be afraid of humans (Genesis 9:2-3). But the righteous king will usher in a state of harmony, returning the world to the ideal that God intended in the beginning. This is developed further by the statement that a child will play on a snake's den, even going so far as to reach inside, but the snake will not harm the child. This reverses Genesis 3:16, where God tells the snake that his offspring and that of humans would strike at each other. But the righteousness established by this king will be so effective that all opposition between humans and nature will be reversed. As a result, there will be no hurt on God's holy mountain, Jerusalem – the site of God's temple and the king's palace. When the king and the LORD function together properly, the result is true knowledge of God, resulting in peace and harmony throughout the world.

This passage presents a portrait of the ideal king. In many ways, he is the opposite of the kind of ruler Samuel warned the people about in 1 Samuel 8 (see Chapter 2 above). Rather than bring about oppression and exploitation, as Samuel said a king would do, his concern for the poor and the meek establishes a state of harmony, like the Garden of Eden before it was lost through sin. This demonstrates that kingship in and of itself is not a bad thing, although Samuel's warning still reminds us that it can easily lead to a negative state of affairs. But at the same time, the desire for a good king in this passage reflects an underlying dissatisfaction with the existing king. People do not usually long for something else if they are satisfied with what they have. By proclaiming Hezekiah as a model king, the prophet is implying that Ahaz, whom Hezekiah replaced, did not live up to that model.

Unfortunately, Hezekiah proved an exception to the rule. As noted earlier, he was one of only three kings who received a positive evaluation in the Bible. The poor leadership by most kings of Israel and Judah ultimately led to the conquest of the northern kingdom by the Assyrians in 721 BCE and of the south by the Babylonians in 587 BCE. The Babylonians went so far as to destroy God's "holy mountain," Jerusalem, even tearing down the Temple itself. After that, this passage took on even greater significance, as the people hoped that just such a ruler would appear again to re-establish the earlier harmonious state of affairs. In time, the terms "branch" and "shoot" (Isaiah 11:1) became code terms for the messiah, a future righteous king who would rule justly (see Jeremiah 23:5; Zechariah 3:8; 6:12).

In the same way, this passage has continued relevance for us today. The ideal it contains can inspire us to desire and even insist on leaders who promote a society marked by justice and equity for the poor and the meek. Although a state of paradise will probably always remain an ideal, it is still an ideal for which we can hope and strive. Having such a goal firmly in mind will help ensure that we do not settle for less. Humans alone cannot bring about heaven on earth. Ultimately, that will require divine intervention. But we can and should anticipate that result, and demand that our leaders act accordingly. Until we experience paradise among us, this text inspires us to hope for something better than what we have.

# 13

## Devouring Leaders:
## "Should you not know justice?"
### Micah 2–3

Micah, a contemporary of Isaiah, prophesied towards the end of the eighth
century BCE. He shared Isaiah's concern for
injustice in the southern kingdom of Judah,
but unlike his more famous colleague, he had a
different perspective toward the rulers of Judah
and the capital city of Jerusalem. Isaiah lived
in Jerusalem but Micah was from Moresheth, a
small village about 40 kilometres southwest of
Jerusalem. He and his fellow villagers did not
reap any benefit from Judah's period of prosperity, but rather were the primary recipients

of the injustice practised by the upper class in Jerusalem. As a result, his reaction to the exploitive practices of the nation's leaders was harsher than that of Isaiah, and he was also much more negative about Jerusalem's fate than Isaiah was.

Micah 2–3 consists of a series of exchanges among Micah, the Judean leaders and the LORD. The speakers are not always explicitly identified or introduced, but it is possible to recognize who is speaking on the basis of what each says. Micah 2 begins with the word *hôy*, which we have already seen in connection with both Amos and Isaiah (see Chapters 8, 10 and 11 above). As we know from those previous chapters, *hôy* indicates that Micah is uttering a funeral lament that focuses on their deeds. And just as with the earlier prophets, their deeds are negative ones.

Micah identifies those whose funeral he is anticipating as people who lie in bed planning "evil deeds" and then put them into effect once the daytime arrives. They do so, Micah says, "because it is in their power" (Micah 2:1)

– an indication that Micah is addressing the powerful members of Israelite society, those in control of the government in Jerusalem. He then goes on in verse 2 to specify just what their "evil deeds" are, in terms that are well known to us from the prophets we have already considered. These people covet their neighbours' fields, seizing the property of those nearby, which Micah characterizes as "oppression" in the second half of the verse. The term "covet" reminds us of the last of the Ten Commandments, which orders the Israelites not to desire their neighbours' possessions. The commandment not to covet reflects the very core of the Covenant relationship. The other commandments all deal with external actions that others can observe and therefore punish. Moreover, the Sixth Commandment had already forbidden adultery and the Seventh Commandment outlawed theft, so the commandment not to covet must deal with something more than those actions. Coveting is a matter of intention. Coveting means to desire what someone else has, regardless of whether you act upon that desire. Coveting another's wife or property would violate the ideal of the Covenant, which was to respect the rights of others. If we persist in desiring what rightfully belongs to another, then we have already broken the Covenant relationship with that person. By including the prohibitions against coveting, the Ten Commandments remind us that the Covenant is not just a matter of actions but very much a matter of attitude. Even if we never act on such desires, when we spend any significant amount of time wishing we had another's property then we have, in effect, broken the Covenant with that person.

In Micah 2:4, the prophet introduces the LORD's response to their actions. People will sing a lament over them, just as the prophet had implied through the use of the word *hôy*. Furthermore, the LORD announces the punishment for their crimes, which ironically will include the land that they have stolen from their neighbours being parcelled out to their own conquerors. The wicked do not repent, but instead order Micah not to preach such things.

They do not intend to change their ways, but they do not want to be confronted with their actions or told of the consequences that await them. Micah responds by reminding them that the LORD's message is a source of "good to one who walks uprightly" (v. 7), but their objection to his words demonstrates that they are not "upright." The prophet contrasts them with their victims: God's own peaceful people (v. 8), especially the women and children (v. 9). He also notes the kind of preaching that the leaders prefer: encouragement to drink alcohol (v. 11). These people are much like those condemned in Amos 6 (see Chapter 8 above), and probably the same group that Isaiah denounced in Isaiah 5:11-12 (see Chapter 10 above).

The prophet gets more explicit, and more graphic, in Micah 3. In verse 1 he makes it clear that he is, in fact, addressing the rulers of the nation. More important, he reminds them that they are supposed to "know justice" – to be aware of what it calls for and ensure that it is carried out. The powerful members of Isra-elite society were responsible for ensuring that the weak are protected; that is what "justice" means in this context. But instead of fulfilling their responsibility to ensure that society is organized justly, they "hate the good and love evil" (Micah 3:2). As a result, Micah compares them to cannibals: they treat people like food, ripping off their skin, stripping the meat from the bones and cooking it in a pot like stew to be eaten. While not meant literally, this is a very graphic image that drives home the point that their treatment of the poor consumes their lives as surely as if they really were cannibals eating their neighbours.

Micah 3:5-7 criticizes other prophets for their failure to speak out against this injustice. Instead, they were motivated by their own gain. They hired themselves out and spoke what their employers wanted to hear – "Peace" – but presented only a negative message ("war") to those who did not pay for their services. Rather than being God's messengers, they sold themselves to the highest bidder and changed their message accordingly. In contrast, Micah holds himself up as a true prophet who speaks in the power and spirit of God, calling for justice and denouncing transgressions against it (Micah 3:8).

Micah 3 culminates with a series of criticisms levelled against those who were charged with ensuring that Israelite society was characterized by the justice that the LORD required. In verses 9 to 10, the prophet denounces the rulers once again for their lack of justice, going so far as to say that their capital city of Jerusalem is built with blood and wrongdoing. In verse 11, Micah includes them as one of three groups condemned for exercising their appointed task for money: the rulers take bribes in the law courts, while the priests teach and the prophets prophesy only when they are paid (we can assume that the latter two do so in such a way that was pleasing to their employers). What is worse, they presume that the LORD is still on their side and will protect them from any and all enemies.

What they fail to realize is that through their injustice they have become God's enemies. Therefore, Micah announces the ultimate

punishment: Jerusalem itself will be destroyed
and the mountaintop where the Temple (i.e.,
"the house [of the LORD]") stood would become
overgrown with trees (3:12). This was a radical
statement in light of the Temple's importance
in Israelite religion and the traditions associated with it. The Temple was considered God's
dwelling place on Earth. The Israelites believed
that the LORD was physically present there,
and therefore that the LORD would intervene
directly if Jerusalem was ever attacked. This had
been a major element in Isaiah's preaching. For
instance, when Judah was attacked by northern
Israel and Syria in 734 BCE, Isaiah told King
Ahaz not to rely on military aid from other
nations but simply to trust in God's protection
of Jerusalem (see, e.g., Isaiah 7:4, 7, 9; 8:10).
Similarly, when Jerusalem was besieged by Sen-
nacherib of Assyria in 701 BCE, Isaiah assured
King Hezekiah that the LORD would protect
the city by fighting on its behalf (e.g., Isaiah
29:5-8; 30:15, 27-33; 31:4-5, 8-9).

Against this background, Micah's shocking
announcement reflects how different Micah's

situation was from Isaiah's. As a resident of
Jerusalem, and perhaps even a member of the
royal family or at least of the royal court, Isaiah
had an attachment to the capital that his rural
contemporary Micah did not share. Because
he lived in the country, Micah was better
able to see the crushing effects of the policies
practised by Judah's rulers, and that Jerusalem
as it existed in his time was, in fact, based on
injustice. Because he believed passionately
that justice was a central aspect of the LORD's
plan for how the nation was to be run, he was
also able to see that it would be necessary for
Jerusalem, the seat and the source of much injustice, to be destroyed in order for true justice
to be embodied in the land. It would be almost
150 years before Micah's prediction came
to pass, when the Babylonians (from what is
southern Iraq today) conquered Jerusalem and
destroyed the Temple in 587 BCE. But Micah's
words were remembered and passed on, so that
when Jeremiah made a similar pronouncement
shortly before the event, people defended him

by quoting Micah's words (see Jeremiah 26:18 and Chapter 15 below).

Institutions and the traditions associated with them can be very powerful things. When those traditions are linked to specific buildings, those buildings take on great symbolic significance. The political capital of a nation is one such symbolic location; when it is attacked, even verbally, that can stir up strong feelings. When it is threatened with physical destruction, the emotional reaction is much more extreme. It is easy to imagine the response if the fourth plane hijacked on September 11, 2001, had not crashed in Pennsylvania but rather had hit what many presume was its target: the White House. The national and international shock and outrage would have been much greater than what did occur after that horrible day.

Now imagine that the political capital was also the religious centre of the nation. That's what Jerusalem was for ancient Israel. The nation's two focal points were combined in a single city. As a result, Micah's pronouncement tore at the very core of their self-understanding as a nation and as a religion. But that was his intent. He made what would have been considered an outrageous and unacceptable prediction in order to shock them, in the hope that they would stop to consider how serious their offence must be if the LORD was willing to destroy the Temple as punishment. If God was willing to attack God's own house, then there must be something seriously wrong with the current state of affairs. There *was* something seriously wrong, and other prophets had named the injustice that characterized the nation, but no one had gone as far as Micah in pointing out the consequences if the people did not change their ways.

What institutions and buildings have the same significance to us? What would it take to make us recognize the injustice within our countries? The Canadian Parliament buildings in Ottawa or Buckingham Palace in London? St. Peter's Basilica or Westminster Cathedral? Perhaps some attach the greatest significance to a sports arena or a mega-mall. Whatever it is, consider how we would react if it were gone, or even just threatened. And then consider whether we allow that place to lull us into not recognizing how we fall short of what God requires of us.

# 14

# GOD'S LAWSUIT:
## "HE HAS TOLD YOU WHAT IS GOOD"
### Micah 6:1-8

In Micah 6, the LORD enters into a lawsuit with the people of Israel, a technique often used by the prophets to challenge the people's complacency. The Israelites were familiar with lawsuits in their ordinary dealings with one another, so it was a metaphor they would easily understand. Moreover, since a major part of their shortcomings was injustice, it made sense to address the matter in a symbolic law court.

The LORD announces the lawsuit itself in verses 1 to 2, calling the mountains and hills to serve as witnesses and judges between the LORD and the people. The mountains are frequently invoked for this purpose in the First Testament, especially in divine lawsuits, because mountains are the "enduring foundations of the earth" (Micah 6:2). They have existed since creation, and thus serve three purposes. First, they are ancient, and since wisdom is linked with age, they symbolize the insight needed to judge the case appropriately. Second, because they have existed from of old, they would have witnessed all the interactions between the LORD and Israel. Finally, since they are made of rock the mountains and hills are a symbol of dispassionate testimony and judgment.

In Micah 6:3-5, the LORD asks what he has done to Israel to cause them to "weary" of him. This statement indicates that they have broken their relationship with God. However, the LORD still considers them "my people" (v. 3), which was a basic element of the Covenant (see Chapter 1 above); such language indicates that the LORD has maintained his side of the Covenant, even though they have turned away.

The next two verses review some of God's past dealings as examples of his care and protection. In the Exodus, God intervened on behalf of Israel when they were in Egypt, setting them free from "the house of slavery." Moreover, the LORD did not just liberate them and then abandon them to make their own way. Instead, he sent them Moses, Aaron and Miriam to be their leaders and guides. Moses confronted Pharaoh, demanding that Pharaoh let the Israelites go, led them to Sinai to receive the laws from God that established the Covenant, then led them through the desert to the edge of the Promised Land. When they repeatedly complained during their time in the wilderness, Moses intervened on their behalf with the LORD, convincing God not to abandon them despite their lack of faith and trust. Aaron and Miriam, Moses' brother and sister, also helped the people. Aaron, as the High Priest, officiated at their worship, and Miriam, as a prophetess, conveyed God's word to the people and the people's praise to God.

Verse 5 moves on to the episode of Balak and Balaam. Numbers 22 to 24 narrates how King Balak of Moab (central Jordan today) feared that the Israelites would eliminate his own people, or at least occupy all the neighbouring territory. In response, he sent for a non-Israelite prophet named Balaam to curse Israel. God told Balaam not to go or to curse the Israelites, because God had, in fact, blessed them. But Balaam disobeyed and went with the Moabite messengers, so God sent a heavenly messenger to warn Balaam to speak only the words that God gave to him. As a result, when Balaam arrived at the southern border of Moab with Balak, every time he opened his mouth, Balaam pronounced a blessing over the Israelites. When Balak complained, Balaam could only reply, "Must I not take care to say what the LORD puts into my mouth?" (Numbers 23:12; see also Numbers 23:25; 24:12-13).

This was not the only time that the LORD protected Israel during their journey from Egypt to the Holy Land. Verse 5 also refers to Shittim and Gilgal. The episode at Shittim is narrated in Numbers 25:1-9. After the episode with Balak and Balaam, the Israelite men had sexual relations with Moabite women, who in turn invited the Israelites to their sacrificial feasts devoted to the Moabite gods. God sent a plague (Numbers 25:8) as punishment, leading Moses and Phineas to execute the offenders. This is a gruesome tale, although not unusual according to the customs of all ancient peoples. But for our purposes we should note three things: (1) the people were quick to turn away from the LORD immediately after God had protected them; (2) Moses and Phineas acted to appease God's anger; and (3) God ultimately forgave them despite their ingratitude and sin.

The second place mentioned in Micah 6:5 is Gilgal, which refers to an incident found in Joshua 4:19-24. Joshua 3:1–4:18 describes how the Israelites crossed the Jordan River just like they crossed the Sea of Reeds (the "Red Sea" is a mistranslation of the original Hebrew) at the time of the Exodus. After Joshua tells the people that they will see God's power, the

Jordan River stopped flowing, with the water from the north piling up into a wall while the water to the south continued to drain into the Dead Sea. The people crossed the river on dry land, just as a generation earlier their ancestors had crossed the Sea of Reeds to escape the pursuing Egyptian army. This time, however, they were not in danger, since God had already prevented Balaam from cursing them, and therefore Balak, the King of Moab, had not been able to defeat them. Instead, Joshua promised them that the LORD would protect them against the inhabitants of the land they were about to enter (Joshua 3:10).

The physical sign of this promise is significant. Whereas Moses had raised his staff over the sea to part the waters (Exodus 14:16, 21), Joshua sent twelve priests, one from each of the tribes, to carry the Ark of the Covenant into the Jordan River. When they reached the river's edge, the water stopped. The priests stood with the Ark in the middle of the dry riverbed as the people crossed over. The Ark of the Covenant was a sign of God's ongoing protection. But they had to follow the Covenant itself if they wanted that protection to continue.

After the people had crossed the Jordan River and the priests brought the Ark of the Covenant up out of the riverbed, the water began to flow again. Then the people camped at Gilgal, on the Israel side of the river. Joshua took twelve stones that he had gathered from the bed of the river and set them up in a pile. They were to serve as a permanent reminder of what had happened there, so that the people would not forget how the LORD had helped them on their journey, and so that they would remain faithful to God forever.

But they obviously had not remained faithful, since the LORD had now entered into a lawsuit against them. Still, this reminder of their past dealings with God evidently worked. In Micah 6:6-7, the people asked what they needed to do in order to be reconciled with God, and their suggestions became increasingly more extravagant. They started with burnt offerings of year-old calves. This common sacrifice in Israelite religion expressed one's devotion by burning the entire animal, unlike most sacrifices, in which only a portion was offered to God and the rest was shared by the worshipper's family and friends. But they went on to suggest that more extreme measures were needed to restore the relationship with the LORD. First, they asked if the quantity of sacrifices should be greatly multiplied: perhaps it would take thousands of animals, or even ten thousand *rivers* of oil to satisfy the LORD? Or maybe God required the sacrifice of their firstborn before forgiving their sin?

But Israel's religious laws already indicated what kinds of sacrifice were called for in various situations, and there is no indication that multiplying the number of items offered was any more effective than offering a single one. More important, in Micah 6:7 they even think that child sacrifice might be necessary, and even worse, desired by the LORD! This shows that the people have completely missed the point. The story about Abraham trying to sacrifice Isaac in Genesis 22 demonstrated that the LORD does *not* desire child sacrifice, unlike some of the neighbouring gods. Moreover, although the laws required that the firstborn of all living creatures were to be dedicated to the LORD, they also specified that in the case of human beings, they are to be "redeemed" or bought back (see Exodus 13:13; Numbers 18:15). Similarly, the Levites were dedicated to the LORD's service in place of sacrificing the children (e.g., Numbers 3:12, 41; 45.).

In response to this outrageous suggestion, Micah 6:8 reminds the people that they have already been told what is good, and what the LORD requires of them: "to do justice, and to love kindness, and to walk humbly with your God." It is no secret what the LORD wanted; in fact, it has already been communicated to them. Micah 6:8 is a summary of the three prophets who were active just before or at the same time of Micah himself. The call for justice echoes Amos's constant message, while the term "kindness" translates *chesed*, a central term in Hosea's call for fidelity to the Covenant (see Chapter 9 above). Isaiah repeatedly urged Israel's kings to trust humbly in God's protective presence rather than in foreign military power (see especially Isaiah 7:9; 30:15); Micah summarizes this as "walk humbly with your God." Through this appeal to the messages of his prophetic colleagues, Micah reminds the people both that their violation of the Covenant is not new, and that they have repeatedly been warned and told what to do. While sacrifice is a valuable act of piety, it is no substitute for the positive actions towards others that the LORD has asked of them.

We have an even greater advantage than those whom Micah addressed. We have the same resources to which he alluded: namely, the history of God's intervention on behalf of those in need, the laws conveying the requirements of the Covenant the LORD offers us, and the testimony of Amos, Hosea and Isaiah (and now Micah) as to what that means in concrete terms for our daily life. We also have the 2,700 years of scripture and tradition since then that have continuously called believers to a life marked by justice, concern and humility. Later prophets also challenged the people to abide by the Covenant; Jesus regularly reminded his followers of the need to care for one another; Paul emphasized the need to love both God and one another (Romans 13:8-10); 1 John 4:20-21 speaks of how impossible it is to love the God we do not see if we do not love the neighbour that we do see; and James 5:1-6 rebukes the rich who did not act justly (see also James 2:1-8, 15-17). Such examples could be greatly multiplied from the scriptures and from the teaching of Jewish and Christian leaders (to say nothing of those from other traditions) throughout the centuries.

Yes, we have been told far more than Micah's audience "what is good, and what does the LORD require of you." Our task is to live it out in our daily lives.

# JEREMIAH'S TEMPLE SERMON: "HAS THIS HOUSE BECOME A DEN OF ROBBERS?"

### Jeremiah 7

Jeremiah prophesied 100 years after Isaiah and Micah, from about 627 BCE until sometime after the Babylonian destruction of Jerusalem in 587 BCE. He was a priest from the village of Anathoth, about 5 kilometres northeast of Jerusalem, but most of his preaching was done in Jerusalem itself. However, his hometown suggests that he came from a long line of important priests. Abiathar, one of two High Priests under David, was exiled to Anathoth by Solomon (1 Kings 2:26-27). Abiathar himself was descended from Eli, the Israelite priest at Shiloh when Samuel received his call to be a prophet (1 Samuel 3). Thus, Jeremiah appears to have had a long and impressive lineage, and the traditions associated with his priestly ancestors played a role in shaping his message to Israel.

Jeremiah lived during a period of increasing threat to Israel from external sources. The Babylonians, who were centred in what is now southern Iraq, had taken over the Assyrian Empire, and so the southern kingdom of Judah was a vassal to the Babylonians. Many Israelites thought that the LORD would deliver them from their overlords, but Jeremiah considered the Babylonians to be God's instrument, sent to punish the Israelites for their sins. As such, the prophet thought defeat was inevitable. Resisting the Babylonians was the same as trying to resist the LORD; neither was possible, so it was better to surrender. This was the situation when Jeremiah preached his "temple sermon" recorded in Jeremiah 7 (with another version in Jeremiah 26).

God told Jeremiah to stand at the entrance
to the Temple in Jerusalem and tell the people
of Judah who entered, "Amend your ways and
your doings" (Jeremiah 7:3). Lest there be any
confusion as to what was required, he did not
tell them just to "repent" or "convert." Although
Israel's history had repeatedly shown them
that repentance could not be separated from
actions, it is always possible for someone to
ignore that fact and think conversion is only an
internal matter that did not have to affect one's
behaviour. We learn from subsequent verses
that the people had done precisely that – di-
vorced their worship from their actions – and
therefore Jeremiah needed to call for a concrete
change. Only if the people changed their ways
would the LORD dwell with them "in this place,"
i.e., in the Temple.

In other words, Jeremiah was saying that
the LORD was not actually present in the Temple
at that time. This is a direct contradiction of
Israelite tradition, which considered the Temple to be God's dwelling place on earth, the
location from which the divine presence spread

through the land. Moreover, we saw earlier in
Chapter 12 that Isaiah had appealed directly to
this tradition when he urged King Ahaz and,
later, King Hezekiah to trust only in the LORD.
In both instances, Isaiah promised them that
the LORD would not merely protect Jerusalem,
but even fight directly against the armies that
threatened it. When Hezekiah believed and
trusted in this promise, the mighty Assyrian
army failed to overcome the city (see 2 Kings
19:32-37). As a result, the Israelite belief that
God would protect them was strengthened.

By the time of Jeremiah, however, many
had separated their belief in God's protective
presence in the Temple from the need to live
according to God's commands. Instead, they
had come to believe that God's protection
would be given automatically, no matter how
they lived. This is reflected in Jeremiah 7:4,
where Jeremiah tells them, "Do not trust in
these deceptive words: 'This is the temple of
the LORD, the temple of the LORD, the temple
of the LORD.'" The emphasis would probably
have been on the words "the LORD." It is not

just because there was a temple in Jerusalem, but rather that it was *the LORD's* temple that produced a protective power. Moreover, they repeated the phrase three times, as if the words themselves had some kind of magical power. But Jeremiah says that such words are "deceptive." The people had deluded themselves into thinking that God was with them no matter what.

In Jeremiah 7:5-6, the prophet indicates where they have gone wrong. He begins with the general statement that they do not act justly with one another, then specifies what he means. First, they oppress the alien, the orphan and the widow. We have already seen that the alien, the orphan and the widow are frequently singled out for protection because they do not have Israelite relatives to protect their rights. The admonitions to protect orphans and widows are often connected with the Exodus from Egypt, and the plight of the alien is compared to the Israelites' situation when they were strangers in Egypt and enslaved. Second, they have shed "innocent blood." This is condemned

frequently in the First Testament (e.g., Deuteronomy 19:10; 27:25; Proverbs 1:11; 6:17;
Isaiah 59:7), because killing someone who has
done no wrong is especially abhorrent. In sum,
the Israelites have violated their own traditions
that call for the protection of specific groups
of individuals. Jeremiah links this to their worship of other gods, and repeats that only if they
cease such things will the LORD "dwell with you
in this place" (Jeremiah 7:7).

But he does not consider this likely, because
they trust in "deceptive words to no avail,"
(Jeremiah 7:8) repeating the phrase from verse
4. Once again, the words are deceptive and
not useful because of their actions. They have
broken at least four of the Ten Commandments
– those against stealing, murder, adultery and
false oaths (Jeremiah 7:9), and have offered
sacrifices to Baal and worshipped other foreign
gods. Then, to make matters worse, they return
to the LORD's own Temple, the one "called by
my name," and think they are safe from foreign
threats. The Temple has become a source of
automatic protection in their minds. But in

God's mind it has become a "den of robbers" (Jeremiah 7:11; cited by Jesus in Matthew 21:13). This phrase says more about them than about the Temple. Jeremiah is not condemning the Temple itself as a place of robbery, because robbers do not practise their trade in their own dens. Rather, robbers retreat to their den after they have robbed. In the same way, the people retreat to the Temple after their acts of injustice and idolatry, thinking that simply by being there they will be safe from harm, because they think that God *must* protect them whenever they are in the LORD's house.

To correct them, Jeremiah points to an event from his own family history: the destruction of Shiloh (vv. 12-15). Shiloh, located about 29 kilometres north of Jerusalem, was the first Israelite sanctuary established in the land (Jerusalem did not become part of Israel until King David captured the city; see 2 Samuel 5:6-9). The Ark of the Covenant was placed there, and it was there that Samuel was dedicated to the Lord and received his call to be the first prophet in Israel (1 Samuel 1–3). But despite its importance, Shiloh did not remain the central sanctuary. The Philistines captured the Ark after it was taken into battle, and when they returned it, the Ark was taken to Kiriath-Jearim rather than to Shiloh (see 1 Samuel 4–7). The Bible does not state explicitly that the Philistines conquered Shiloh (although see Psalm 78:60-64), but archaeology reveals that the city was destroyed around that time. Shiloh's fate indicates that if the LORD could destroy one place of worship because of sin, he could certainly do it again if the people continued their injustice and idolatry. Therefore, they should not put any special trust in the Jerusalem temple in and of itself.

Many people would have considered Jeremiah's words to be blasphemous, and at a time when the nation's survival was at stake, perhaps treasonous as well. We know from Jeremiah 26:8 and 11 that many wanted to put him to death after this, but others saved him by appealing to the prediction in Micah 3:12 more than a century earlier that Jerusalem would someday be destroyed (see Jeremiah 26:16-19). Nonetheless, Jeremiah was arrested and imprisoned on other occasions because of his preaching (see Jeremiah 32:4-5; 37:15-16; 38:4-6) and, according to ancient traditions not preserved in the Bible, he was killed by some Israelites who had forced him to go with them to Egypt after Jerusalem was destroyed.

Jeremiah's Temple Sermon reminds us that our modern places of worship should not always make us feel comfortable. Certainly there are times when comfort is what we need, such as in times of personal loss or spiritual difficulty. Coming together with other believers, hearing God's word proclaimed and celebrating God's presence among us can be a source of great consolation. Communal worship is meant to bring us closer to God. But there may be other times when we must first be challenged to change our ways, just as Jeremiah's audience needed to be challenged. Few will be guilty of the sins Jeremiah lists, but if we think that we never stray from the way that God wants us to live, then we are fooling ourselves just as surely as Jeremiah's audience did. We must expect the liturgy to shake us up once in while, causing us to reflect on whether we could do a better job of embodying the Covenant outside of church as well.

This passage also gives us a model of someone who spoke the LORD's word, no matter how shocking his audience found his words or the threat to his own life. There are many examples of such clarity of purpose today as well, from national and international church leaders to local community workers who are willing to challenge the injustices that continue to plague our society. These voices are often dismissed, and sometimes attacked, but they persist. We must each consider how we might do the same, in whatever way and on whatever scale we can.

## 16

### TRUE KNOWLEDGE OF THE LORD:
### "IS NOT THIS TO KNOW ME?"

**Jeremiah 22:13-19**

Like other prophets before him, Jeremiah knew how to use the funeral lament to communicate his prophetic message. This oracle begins with the Hebrew word *hôy* ("woe" in the NRSV), which marked the beginning of a eulogy for someone who had died (see Chapter 8 above). In keeping with the nature of the *hôy* utterance, the person being mourned is identified not by name but rather by actions. Those actions give us some clues about his identity, clues that are confirmed when Jeremiah 22:18 specifies that the prophet is speaking of King

Jehoiakim, who ruled Judah from 609–598 BCE.

This "Woe Oracle" begins by noting that this person "builds his house by iniquity." Since Jeremiah 22:1 and 11 both introduce oracles about kings of Judah, at first glance we might think that "house" here refers to a royal dynasty, but the second line of verse 13 clarifies that it is an actual building. Moreover, the presence of "upper rooms" indicates that this is no ordinary home, since only the wealthy could afford two-storey buildings. Verse 14 provides even more detail: the house is spacious; it has large upper rooms, windows (not a common feature in the ancient world), cedar panelling and bright paint. This is clearly a mansion, and perhaps even a palace. That possibility is even more likely because of the terms "unrighteousness" and "injustice" in verse 13, which echo the call in Jeremiah 22:3 for the King of Judah to "act with justice and righteousness." (Note also the concern for "the alien, the orphan and the widow" as well as "innocent blood" in v. 3, and compare them with Jeremiah 7:6.) Moreover, the last two lines of Jeremiah 22:13 tell us that this individual has built his home with forced labour, without compensation. This is exactly what Samuel warned the people a king would do (see 1 Samuel 8:17 and Chapter 2 above).

Any doubt that Jeremiah was addressing a king is removed in verse 15, where Jeremiah asks what makes him a king? Is it his opulent lifestyle, exemplified by his use of cedar? No. For Jeremiah, a true king of Judah is identified by his actions. Jeremiah 22:3-4 states that a king must "act with justice and righteousness"; if he does not, then the LORD will remove him from David's throne. In verse 15, Jeremiah makes this specific by referring to the current king's father. Verse 18 tells us that the prophet was addressing Jehoiakim, son of Josiah. Out of all the kings who ruled in Israel or Judah, only three receive a positive evaluation in the Books of Kings, and Josiah was one of them (2 Kings 22:2; 23:25; the other two were Asa [1 Kings 15:11-14] and Hezekiah [2 Kings 18:3-7]. Thus, Josiah was a positive model of kingship, especially to his own son.

Jeremiah acknowledged that Josiah lived like a king: he ate and drank, indicating a life with some degree of comfort. But Josiah also did "justice and righteousness," as required of the king in Jeremiah 22:3. The result was that "Then it was well with him" (Jeremiah 22:15). There is a direct connection between Josiah's positive actions and his own state of well-being. Verse 16 elaborates on what Jeremiah meant by "justice and righteousness": Josiah "judged the cause of the poor and the needy." This is exactly what we would expect, in keeping with the overall expectations of the First Testament. The result of those specific acts of "justice and righteousness" was that "then it was well." This phrase in verse 16 repeats some words from verse 15, with a small but important difference. The first time, Josiah's general practice of justice resulted in a positive outcome for himself. The second time, because he protected the needy members of the nation in particular, "it was well," not just for him but in general. When the nation's leader acted on behalf of those most in need of assistance, the nation as a whole experienced a positive result, because that is precisely how the LORD wants the society to be organized: with the weak being cared for by the strong.

Jeremiah 22:16 ends with an interesting question. After describing Josiah's practice of justice in both general and specific terms, followed by the result for both himself and the community as a whole, Jeremiah adds, "'Is not this to know me?' says the LORD." The prophet draws a direct connection between justice and righteousness on the one hand, and knowledge of God on the other, indicating that they are the same. One comes to know God by *acting* justly. This differs from most concepts of knowledge in Western society. Most of us view knowledge as something that comes through thinking and reflection, or at least by reading what others have thought. But in ancient Israel, knowledge came from experience. Knowing something meant that you had encountered it directly. The same applied to knowledge of a person. Jeremiah is saying that knowledge of God, in the Israelite sense of experiencing God,

is the same as acting with justice and righteousness. We encounter God when we act justly.

The reason for this is that acting justly
is a fundamental aspect of God's own being.
As noted in Chapter 1 above, the Exodus was
central to Israel's relationship with the LORD
and is referred to throughout the First Testament. Only after the Exodus did the LORD give
them the Covenant laws that laid out how
the people were to relate to God, and in turn
to one another. Many of the laws themselves
were rooted in the importance of establishing
a way of life together that was radically different from what they had experienced as slaves
in Egypt. Similarly, the prophets consistently
appealed to the Exodus as the basis for their
message of conversion and renewal (e.g., Isaiah
10:26; 11:16; Jeremiah 2:6; 11:4; Ezekiel 20:5-
6; Hosea 11:1; Amos 2:10; 3:1; Micah 6:4;
Haggai 2:5). As a people, the Israelites came
to know the LORD in and through the LORD's
intervention on behalf of a group of slaves. The
Israelites' foundational experience was of a God
who acted for the benefit of the weak and needy

members of society. And if knowledge comes through doing, then the best way to know God was to act the way God acts.

After this pronouncement about how one truly knows God, Jeremiah 22:17 reinforced how much Jehoiakim had fallen short. Instead of acting like his father, he was interested only in "dishonest gain." As a result, he shed "innocent blood," in direct violation of numerous commands through the First Testament, including Jeremiah's own words in Jeremiah 22:3. Jehoiakim also practised "oppression and violence," even though in verse 3 Jeremiah had told the King of Judah (the king is unnamed, but the message applies to Jehoiakim as well as to other kings) to deliver people from "the oppressor" and not to do "violence." Jeremiah made such things a condition for the king to remain on the throne; by his actions, Jehoiakim has demonstrated that he did not deserve to rule.

Jeremiah's "Woe Oracle" ends with the announcement of Jehoiakim's punishment, which has two elements. The first is that they will not

lament for him when he dies (Jeremiah 22:18).
No one shall say "alas" when he is gone. The
Hebrew word is the same one that is translated
as "woe" in verse 13: *hôy*. Jeremiah ironically
utters a funeral lament about Jehoiakim while
he is alive in order to indicate that the king will
not receive one at the time of his death. That
is because he will not receive a proper burial;
instead, his body will be thrown out the city
gates like that of a donkey. The second element
of Jehoiakim's punishment is that he will be remembered for the deeds that Jeremiah laments
in this passage, and so there will be no basis for
anyone to praise him at his death.

What if our leaders took Jeremiah's words
to heart? What would modern societies look
like if those in power planned their actions
according to Jeremiah's criteria for a good
king? Some say we cannot help the poor or
the needy because it is not practical, or we do
not have the resources, or for similar reasons.
We often hear about the need to balance the
national budget or how this or that policy will
adversely affect the economy. But Jeremiah

approached the matter from the other side of things. He started from the perspective of what was necessary to improve the situation of the needy and then demanded that those in power do so. This need not mean sacrificing all good things in life, although it may require some sacrifice, and will result in a better life for everyone. After all, people who spend at least some of their time and resources helping others report a greater sense of personal satisfaction than those who do not.

One way to encourage us to that end is to remember Jeremiah's other major point in this passage: that true knowledge of God comes from acting like God. We are called to more than just abstract knowledge of God. There are many doctrines and beliefs *about* God, and they are important for ensuring that we remain true to the faith that God has revealed. But they are no substitute for an encounter with God's very own self. Knowing *about* God is important for believers, but so is *knowing God* directly.

# 17

# THE GOOD SHEPHERD:
## "I MYSELF WILL BE THE SHEPHERD OF MY SHEEP"

### Ezekiel 34

Ezekiel was a priest who was deported to Babylon in 598 BCE. Jehoiakim had revolted against his Babylonian overlord, who in turn attacked and captured Jerusalem. As punishment for the revolt and to lessen the chances of another rebellion, the Babylonians took many of the leading citizens back with them as hostages. Ezekiel received his call to the prophetic ministry in Babylon in the year 593 BCE. In his first years as a prophet, he called the people in Jerusalem to repentance, but instead the kings rebelled once again. In response, the Babylonian army returned to Judah and destroyed Jerusalem, tearing down the Temple and deporting more of the population.

This devastating event had significant theological implications. In the ancient world, people believed that their gods would protect them from their enemies, so when one nation conquered another nation, people thought that this happened because the god(s) of the victorious nation were more powerful than those of the defeated nation. The ancient Israelites not only shared this view, they also believed that the Temple was the LORD's home, the divine dwelling place on earth. Since the Temple was the focal point of God's presence among the Israelites, they assumed that God would provide it with special protection. And since the Temple was in Jerusalem, that special protection must extend to the city itself. So, when the Babylonians conquered the city, many would have thought that Marduk, the chief god of Babylon, was more powerful than the LORD. It seemed as if the LORD had not even been able to protect his own home, never mind the people of Israel! Thus, many would have been tempted to abandon their faith and worship Marduk instead.

Ezekiel 34 addresses the issue of why the LORD had allowed Jerusalem to be destroyed. Ezekiel wanted to explain their stunning defeat so that the Israelites could retain their faith in the LORD. To that end, Ezekiel blamed the situation on the Israelites themselves, both the leaders and the people. This catastrophe was a result of their failure to care for the needy members of their community, leading to God's punishment through the Exile.

Like other prophets before him, Ezekiel began his oracle with the Hebrew word *hôy*, translated by the NRSV as "Ah" in Ezekiel 34:2, but he also adds something new. What follows is an extended metaphor in which Ezekiel first addressed the shepherds and then the sheep. It is obvious that the shepherds stand for the leaders of the nation and the sheep for the people in general.

A shepherd's job is to look after the flock, making sure that the sheep are fed and protecting them from predators. Instead, these shepherds have been feeding themselves (v. 2). They derived many benefits from the flock: they used the wool for clothing and ate the fatted animals, but they did not feed them (v. 3). Ezekiel 34:4 contains a few subtle reminders that the prophet is really concerned about the people of Israel, and not just animals. While the point he makes could apply to sheep, the shepherds' failure to care for the weak, the sick and injured uses language that usually refers to the Israelites' obligations to one another. Similarly, the failure to look for the sheep that have strayed and become lost is also appropriate to shepherds, but Ezekiel notes that they did not "shepherd" their charges, but rather "ruled them," and did so "with force and harshness" (v. 4). In other words, the leaders have exploited the people as a whole, feeding and clothing themselves through taxes, exploitation and so on.

Because the "shepherds" have not watched over the flock properly, the sheep have become scattered and are easy prey for wild animals (Ezekiel 34:5-8). The wild animals are the Babylonians, who killed many in the battles that led up to the destruction of Jerusalem. The fact that the sheep were scattered refers to the Babylonian Exile itself. Thus, the reason that Jerusalem and the Temple have been destroyed is that the rulers have not exercised their leadership role properly. As a result, the LORD announces that he will care for the sheep himself (Ezekiel 34:11-16). The LORD will seek them out the way a true shepherd should, bringing them back from among the nations into which they have been scattered, and providing them with good pasture. God will do precisely what the shepherds did not do: go in search of the lost and strayed, and care for the injured and the weak (compare v. 16 with v. 4). The final sentence in verse 16 reminds us once again that this is really about human beings, when the LORD says, "I will feed them with justice."

God will give them what the rulers had not: justice.

The LORD also had something to say about the sheep, in Ezekiel 34:17-21. The sheep were not all the same. Some were fat and some were lean, which suggests that the sheep did not share equally in what was available to them. Some had taken the best pasture and water, at the expense of the others (vv. 18-19). That would be bad enough, but they then trampled over the remaining pasture and spoiled the water. This imagery indicates that some members of the general population have also acted unjustly towards the others. They have taken more than their fair share of the community's resources and made it impossible for the others to enjoy what remained. Moreover, they used their power and strength to push the weaker sheep around (v. 21). This is a clear case of the strong exploiting the weak rather than caring for them, as they should have done. So the LORD announced that he would judge the flock according to its actions, and punish those who had become fat while others became lean.

The rest of Ezekiel 34 presents an idyllic picture of the LORD's flock restored to a state of harmony. They will be returned to their land and have plenty of water to drink and food to eat. They will rest as God protects them from the "wild animals" that might seek to attack and enslave them. As a result, they will be free from fear and want. Thus, they will know that God is with them and that they truly are the LORD's people: "'You are my sheep, the sheep of my pasture and I am your God,' says the LORD GOD" (Ezekiel 34:31).

Ezekiel 34 reflects God's ongoing care for the people of Israel during the Babylonian Exile. God did not abandon the people when they were attacked and conquered by the Babylonians, even though their defeat was a direct consequence of their actions. The injustice and exploitation of the people by both the leaders and some of the population resulted in their punishment. But the LORD did not abandon them to their fate. Ezekiel brought a word of hope: they would eventually be restored to their land, and the life of harmony that God desired for them would eventually be theirs.

That message remains relevant today. Unfortunately, there are still those who treat others as objects that exist only to make their own lives easier. Some take the best of what is available with little concern for the fact that this leaves others without enough. This applies both to how the wealth of a single nation is shared among its citizens and to the fact that the developed countries consume a much greater share of the world's resources, leaving the other countries to subsist on less than their fair share. Moreover, global industrial policies often mean that after the few have taken the resources from foreign countries, those countries are left to deal with the pollution and environmental destruction caused by exploitive mining or forestry practices. But just as God judged between the fat and the lean sheep in Ezekiel's day, so too the LORD will hold us responsible for how we have shared our world with the rest of our brothers and sisters. Trampling the pasture of others and soiling their water were unacceptable then, and still are today.

But we can take great comfort from another aspect of this passage: the LORD loves the sheep and cares for them. Just as the LORD sought out those who had become lost, so too God seeks us out when we go astray. The LORD does not abandon people when they are in difficulty, but always seeks to bring them back and restore their lives. At the same time, God wants to set right any imbalance that we have created in the world. All we have to do is co-operate with God's plan. No matter what, we should always remember the words "'I am your God,' says the LORD GOD" (Ezekiel 34:31).

# 18

# THE TRUE FAST

## Isaiah 58

Chapters 56 to 66 of Isaiah date from after the Babylonian Exile. In the previous chapter, I discussed the brutal effects the Exile had on the faith of the conquered Israelites. Despite this difficult time, many kept their faith, both those in exile in Babylon and those left to scrape out a living in their devastated country of Judah. Eventually, the exiles returned from Babylon and, together with those left in the land, sought to rebuild the nation. Because of the lofty preaching of some prophets during the Exile (e.g., Ezekiel 40–48; Isaiah 49:14-23; 54:1-17), they expected to have a place

of importance in the world, with Jerusalem as
the political and religious centre of the ancient
Near East. But that did not happen. They rebuilt the Temple, but Judah was much smaller
than it had been before the Babylonians conquered them. Much of their territory had been
taken over by surrounding nations. To make
things worse, the nation and the people were
no longer independent. Instead, Judah was just
a small part of a larger province in the Persian
Empire (centred in what is Iran today).

As a result, the people complained to God.
They did not understand why they were not
better off. They had rebuilt the Temple and
resumed the sacrifices that were part of their
religion. They performed the religious rituals
that the Law called for. They observed the
Sabbath and the other holy days. But they did
not have the position in the world that they
thought they deserved. They humbled themselves before God, and made sacrifices in their
lives by fasting, and yet God did not seem to
hear or answer (Isaiah 58:3). Why should they
bother to perform religious acts such as fast-

ing if these did not produce positive results in their lives?

In response, the LORD instructed them in the rest of Isaiah 58 concerning the true meaning of fasting. Fasting is not just a matter of external actions but also a matter of the heart. They thought it was enough to perform the usual rituals that accompany fasting, such as putting on sackcloth and sprinkling ashes on themselves as a sign of humility and repentance before God (v. 5). What they failed to realize is that such things are supposed be an external expression of an internal attitude. Without the proper state of mind and heart, those actions were meaningless by themselves. Even worse, other things they did actually separated them from God. While they were fasting, they also oppressed their workers, argued with one another and even resorted to violence (vv. 3-5). Despite their religious activities, their real focus was on their own interests rather than God's. Such fasting can never be acceptable to God.

So the LORD described the kind of fast they should undertake, the kind of fast that God desires. It means doing the opposite of what they had been doing. Once again we learn that what God desires most is a society character- ized by justice and righteousness. If they want to engage in a fast that is pleasing to the LORD, then they need to stop injustice and liberate the oppressed (vv. 6, 9). What this means in real life is spelled out in very concrete terms. They are to feed the hungry, house the homeless and clothe the naked (vv. 7, 10). They must not cut themselves off from their neighbours but rather enter into a relationship with them, especially those most in need.

Doing that would ensure that the Sabbath was properly observed. They concentrated on their own concerns on the Sabbath Day, rather than attending to its true purpose (v. 13). The Sabbath is supposed to be a holy day. In ancient Hebrew, the word we translate as "holy" was linked to the idea of separation, of being set apart. The Sabbath is supposed to be a day that is separate from the other days of the week, a period that is set apart from what concerns us the rest of the week. The Sabbath is a day of rest, but not just in the sense of inaction. It does not mean that we do nothing (other than go to church), but rather that we stop doing the things we do on the other days of the week. By continuing to focus on themselves and their own affairs on the Sabbath, they made it a day just like any other. Despite their religious actions, despite their fasting, they were not behaving any differently than they did on the other six days of the week. Their Sabbath was no different from those other days. It was not "holy," in the sense of being set apart

But what if they were to change? What if they were to enact the true fast desired by the LORD, one in which they acted with justice and cared for the needs of the disadvantaged members of their community? Once again, the result is spelled out quite clearly, in powerful language. Changing their inner attitude will heal their society, removing the oppression that has affected it up until that point (vv. 8-9). As a result, they will become like a light for all to see. Their new way of living in harmony with their neighbours would be like a light in the darkness to the surrounding nations (vv. 8-10). At the same time, because they would be acting in the way God desires, God would be present with them once more (vv. 9, 11). When they fasted without loving their fellow Israelites, God did not hear their prayers; but if they changed and began to care for the needy, then the Lord would once again be in their midst, announcing "Here I am!" (v. 9). This divine presence would be constant, and God would nourish and strengthen them (v. 11). Moreover, the cities that were still in ruins after the Babylonian conquest would be rebuilt as a home for generations (v. 12).

But the most important effect of a change on their part would be the restoration of a proper relationship with God. Yes, the Lord would bless them, healing their society, providing for their physical needs and restoring their cities. But more important than those things would be the change in their attitude to God. They would not do those things because God gave them good things in return, but because they "delight in the Lord" (Isaiah 58:14). Changing their behaviour would lead to a change in their frame of mind. They had acted out of self-interest, which led them to exploit others. But if they began to act in the interest of others, their overall attitude would change. Ultimately, they would work for the good of all because it pleased God, and that would be what they desired more than anything else.

Modern believers perform a variety of religious actions. People act in common during the liturgy on Sunday, doing certain things at certain times as part of their common worship. At the same time there are numerous personal and private devotions. Some people pray certain prayers, such as the rosary or the Jesus Prayer. Catholic churches have the Stations of the Cross on the walls to help people reflect on the passion, death and resurrection of Jesus. And people fast, whether on days set aside by church traditions or on days of their own choosing. All these rituals and personal acts of piety can be positive ways of developing one's spirituality and relationship with God. We must not conclude from Isaiah 58 that things like fasting are wrong in and of themselves. God does not order the people to abandon fasting. Rather, this passage emphasizes the importance of a proper attitude. As long as such actions are performed in the proper spirit, they are beneficial. But if they are done for their own sake, as a substitute for concrete actions for the good of others, then they run the risk of becoming empty rituals that God rejects.

Similarly, we need to consider how we keep the Sabbath. What does it mean today to keep it "holy," to make it different from the other days? In North America, it used to be easy to do this because it was mandated by law. But now, with Sunday shopping legal in most places, keeping the day holy is much harder. Moreover, people are generally busier than people were a generation ago. The combination of demanding jobs, children's activities, socializing and other commitments often makes it difficult to get everything done in six days. Household chores, grocery shopping and other tasks can easily spill over onto Sunday, making it harder to keep the Sabbath holy. But that is all the more reason why we need to do it. The LORD did not institute the Sabbath for its own sake, but for ours. Most people know that the Sabbath exists because God rested on the seventh day (Genesis 2:2-3; Exodus 20:8-11). But it also exists because we need a day of rest. Deuteronomy 5:15 links the Sabbath to the Israelites' time in Egypt. When they were slaves, they did not have a day of rest, so God told them to make sure that they enjoyed one from that point on. The LORD did not free them from Egypt just so they could become enslaved to the concerns of their daily lives. In the same way, it is important that we have one day a week on which we take a break from the things we do the rest of the week. How that happens will differ from person to person, but refusing to get enslaved by the constant "busy-ness" of modern society one day a week will ensure that the Sabbath remains holy.

# 19

# The Year of the Lord's Favour: "He has sent me to bring good news to the oppressed"

### Isaiah 61

In Isaiah 61, the prophet proclaims his mission as established by God. He has been anointed with the spirit of the LORD and sent to the oppressed, the brokenhearted, the captives and prisoners, and those who mourn. These are exactly the people on behalf of whom the prophets regularly spoke. In each of the preceding chapters, we have examined various passages in which the prophets rebuked Israel's leaders for failing to protect those very groups of vulnerable people. In fact, this passage comes from the same general time as Isaiah 58, discussed in the previous chapter. The situation has not changed, however. In Isaiah 58, the LORD did not accept the people's fasting, because some people oppressed the poor and enslaved those in need. The poor and enslaved are also mentioned in Isaiah 61.

But this passage is different from all the other prophetic texts we have looked at so far. This time, a prophet is speaking *to* the oppressed, not about them. He announces comfort to the brokenhearted and those in mourning, and liberty to those who are not free, calling this "the year of the LORD's favour." He also calls it "the day of vengeance of our God," according to the NRSV translation. Unfortunately, this misrepresents the meaning of the Hebrew. While the original word can mean "vengeance," it deals primarily with acting on behalf of someone. While this sometimes requires acting against someone else (thus, "vengeance"), it need not. And even when it does, that is not the point of the action, only a necessary side effect. The emphasis is always on the person (or persons) on whose behalf an individual undertakes this action. That is why Isaiah 61:1 recites a series of actions on behalf of people before identifying those deeds as God's "vengeance." Similarly, the end of verse 2 and the beginning of verse 3 insist that the purpose of God's action is to comfort those who mourn. As a result, it would be better to translate the word as "vindication," as in the New American Bible, or "rescue," as the NRSV suggests in a footnote.

The "year of the LORD's favour" is the Jubilee Year. As we saw in Chapter 1, the Covenant required a Jubilee every 50 years. Debts were to be forgiven, those who had been forced to sell themselves as "debt slaves" were to be set free, and land that had been sold was to be returned to its original owner or that person's descendants. Those requirements are reflected in Isaiah 61:1. The prophet first speaks to "the oppressed." This term often occurs in connection with the poor (e.g., Amos 2:7), so the oppression here is most likely economic in nature, brought about by debt. The oppressed are also called the "brokenhearted," suggesting that they have lost hope of ever escaping from what must have been a long-term situation. Also in verse 1, the captives and prisoners are set free, another feature of the Jubilee Year. Verses 4 and 5 then go on to describe how the people will restore the land and grow food and grapes on it once again.

The reason for God's action on the part of the oppressed and enslaved is clearly stated in verse 8: "For I the LORD love justice, I hate robbery and wrongdoing." We know from Isaiah 58 that some Israelites were guilty of precisely those crimes during this period. Since the situation had not changed, the LORD was now going to intervene directly through the Jubilee Year to establish the justice God so earnestly desires. Those who had been afflicted would be compensated and therefore be glad (v. 7). More important, they would become models of what God desires, such that "they will be called oaks of righteousness" (v. 3). "Righteousness" is regularly used in parallel with "justice" and the oak serves as a symbol of solidity and strength. Also, because the liberated embody the society that God intends, the LORD will make "an everlasting covenant" with them and so the surrounding nations will see that the LORD has truly blessed them (v. 9). This in turn will inspire the other nations to praise God and act in righteousness (v. 11).

Jesus used this passage to inaugurate his ministry. After he had been baptized with the Holy Spirit, he went to the synagogue in Nazareth, read Isaiah 61:1-2, and told his listeners, "Today this scripture has been fulfilled in your hearing" (Luke 4:16-20). He also alluded to this text when John the Baptizer asked if Jesus was the one who was to come (Matthew 11:5; Luke 7:22). Jesus clearly saw himself as sent to "proclaim the good news to the poor," meeting their needs in very concrete terms.

Isaiah 61 illustrates the ongoing need for the Jubilee Year in ancient Israel. Some Israelites were still in need of liberation from economic and social hardship. Unfortunately, people continued to fall into debt, even to the point of selling themselves in order to meet their financial responsibilities. God had com-

manded that the Jubilee Year be observed every
50 years in order to address that very situation,
and sent a series of prophets to remind the
nations' leaders of their obligation to practise
justice during the intervals. Just as recently as
Isaiah 58, the Lord had told them that their fasting was unacceptable because they continued
to oppress and enslave their fellow Israelites
(see Chapter 18 above).

But still the situation endured. In fact,
most scholars doubt that the Jubilee was ever
practised by the Israelites. In response, the
LORD announced that he would take matters
into his own hands. Those in need had to be
helped; if people would not do it, then the
LORD would act directly to ensure that those
in need were cared for, in keeping with the
Jubilee's prescriptions. The principles involved
were too important to go unfulfilled, and if that
could happen only through the hand of God,
then so be it.

By quoting this passage some five hundred
years later, Jesus showed that the Jubilee Year
was still needed in his own time. But he indi-

cated something else as well. Jesus said that the passage was fulfilled in the hearing of his listeners. Isaiah 61 expressed God's intention to intervene directly to ensure justice on earth. But injustice still existed, so God became flesh to act against injustice through the life and teaching of Jesus. Jesus consistently called his listeners to act on behalf of the neediest members of society; ultimately, he gave his own life to illustrate the injustice of a society that would kill someone like him.

The proclamation of the Year of the LORD's Favour resonates today. Some people still suffer under enormous financial burdens, often to the point of near-slavery. The words of the prophets and Jesus continue to challenge believers to do something to correct that situation, and some have responded to the call. As the year 2000 approached, a group called Jubilee 2000 lobbied governments from the prosperous nations to put the principles of the Jubilee Year into effect by cancelling the debt of the world's most impoverished nations. That group has continued its efforts ever since, with some degree of success. Although there is much more that nations can do to help other nations, at least there has been a start.

Individuals also need to respond to the call for justice found throughout the Bible. Even if on a much smaller scale, each of us can act to embody the ideals of justice and compassion for the weaker members of society, reaching out to those in need in our community. If we take scripture seriously as God's word to us today, and not only to the Israelites who lived thousands of years ago, then we need to consider how each of us can take on the role of the prophet in Isaiah 61 "to proclaim the year of the LORD's favour." We must challenge our neighbours to act accordingly, but also remember to do so ourselves. A life based on justice for all would be the best proclamation of all. Then, as a just Israelite society would inspire the surrounding nations (Isaiah 61:9 and 11), so too our individual lives of justice may inspire our neighbours to act justly as well. If that happens, all will enjoy the year of the LORD's favour.

# INDEX OF SCRIPTURE REFERENCES

*Note*: Page numbers in bold indicate the start of a chapter dealing with the corresponding text.

## First Testament

## Second Testament